IN SEARCH OF DERRICK TODD LEE

*The Internet Social Movement
That Made a Difference*

Stan Weeber

University Press of America,® Inc.
Lanham · Boulder · New York · Toronto · Plymouth, UK

Copyright © 2007 by
University Press of America,® Inc.
4501 Forbes Boulevard
Suite 200
Lanham, Maryland 20706
UPA Acquisitions Department (301) 459-3366

Estover Road
Plymouth PL6 7PY
United Kingdom

All rights reserved
Printed in the United States of America
British Library Cataloging in Publication Information Available

Library of Congress Control Number: 2007930027
ISBN-13: 978-0-7618-3841-8 (clothbound : alk. paper)
ISBN-10: 0-7618-3841-4 (clothbound : alk. paper)
ISBN-13: 978-0-7618-3842-5 (paperback : alk. paper)
ISBN-10: 0-7618-3842-2 (paperback : alk. paper)

⊖™ The paper used in this publication meets the minimum
requirements of American National Standard for Information
Sciences—Permanence of Paper for Printed Library Materials,
ANSI Z39.48—1984

Contents

Preface   v

Chapter 1 Introduction   1

Chapter 2 The Baton Rouge Serial Murders: An Overview   5

Chapter 3 A Sense of Injustice Builds   15

Chapter 4 The Birth of the Internet Social Movement in Baton Rouge   29

Chapter 5 The Death of Carrie Lynn Yoder   45

Chapter 6 The Arrest and Trial of Derrick Todd Lee   81

Chapter 7 Aftermath, Analysis and New Directions   89

Bibliography   111

Index   117

Preface

This book is about criminologist Maurice Godwin's Internet social movement, the one that sprang to life when citizens in Baton Rouge, south Louisiana and south Mississippi grew increasingly upset by the slow pace and lack of progress of the multi-jurisdictional Task Force seeking the Baton Rouge serial killer. This is a story of citizen empowerment in a time of crisis. I believe that both scholars and ordinary citizens will be inspired by the way that people in Baton Rouge helped themselves and kept the heat on the investigators until the desired result was obtained.

I am an insider to this movement, having participated and observed it since it first appeared on the Internet beginning in January of 2003. I describe and analyze sociologically the key players, the major controversies and the internal dynamics of the movement that kept pressure on the Task Force up until the arrest of Derrick Todd Lee on May 27, 2003.

In the future, I hope that online social movements will be used by law enforcement as an innovative new tool in fighting crime. Sadly that was not the case in the story told in this book, as officers on the Task Force thought the Internet movement to be simply an annoyance to be ignored and scorned. Police need citizens as their eyes and ears on the street in apprehending criminals, so why cannot online citizens be used for the same purpose? In time, police administrators may see the value of this new source of "information on the street."

Stan Weeber
Lake Charles, Louisiana
March 31, 2007

Chapter 1

Introduction

Are you tired of the way that government is slow in responding to your problems? Do you feel trapped with no way out? Do your neighbors feel the same way? The fact is, there is a way out, one that can get a problem solved with relatively minimal cost.

After reading this book, there will no longer be any need for any citizen of the United States, even in the hurricane ravaged Gulf Coast of Louisiana or Mississippi, to feel politically apathetic or to feel that their input means nothing. This book is the story of how a North Carolina criminologist formed an Internet social movement that empowered the citizens of Baton Rouge, Louisiana to help motivate the authorities to move as quickly as they could to solve the case of the south Louisiana serial killer. By joining this movement, citizens empowered themselves. I believe that all people regardless of their social and educational backgrounds will be inspired by the way that people in Baton Rouge helped themselves and kept the heat on the investigators until the desired result was obtained. In May, 2003, Derrick Todd Lee was arrested, and the long nightmare of women in south Louisiana and south Mississippi was finally over.

My sincere hope is that this book will be well received by people along the Gulf Coast and by "true crime" addicts everywhere. Why? Because it will offer up both the best and worst of human nature: conventional and contentious politics and intrigue; money and corruption; complex forensic evidence; lawyers and trials, and intense media coverage. In other words, it is a human interest story similar to the Laci Peterson case in California, the JonBenet Ramsey case in Colorado, and the case of Natalie Holloway, missing and presumed dead in Aruba. The book thus has a general appeal beyond academe.

The book should also be of interest to professional women in the south and throughout the United States that would welcome information about how to protect themselves from the likes of Derrick Todd Lee and other nontraditional predators. Dr. Godwin relayed to women information via Internet about the topics of sexual violence and stalking, and how women could get the help that they needed.

With more than 60 women still missing in Baton Rouge, there was suspicion that more than one serial killer was on the loose. A second suspect was arrested in 2004, with the prospect of more arrests as many of the missing women cases remain unsolved. Hence, the Baton Rouge serial killer case lives on, even though the media spotlight has dimmed.

I am aware of three other writers that have written about the Baton Rouge case. The editor of Baton Rouge's *City Social* magazine has written a book that provides a useful summary and overview of the case that includes descriptions of the fear level in the city during the hunt for the serial killer.[1] A second writer, Stephanie Stanley, who covered the case for a New Orleans newspaper, writes about the case from the perspective of a journalist who covered the story during the intensive and tense search for the killer.[2] Third, Dr. Maurice Godwin, the multi-tasking criminologist and major figure in this book, has published a book called *Tracker* that hit the market in 2005.[3] His book contains two chapters on the Baton Rouge case. Therefore, the reader will have other sources with which to compare and contrast the analysis that I provide. My book, however, will be the only one that looks in any depth at the Internet social movement that helped in tracking down Derrick Todd Lee. And my take on the subject is one that would differ from that of the others who have written about the Baton Rouge case.

I am a Ph.D. sociologist, and thus I'm in a unique position to make some sociological observations about the Internet movement and the case as a whole. I participated in and observed the social movement being described in this book, and I consider myself to be knowledgeable of the topic of social movements in general. I have contributed over 70 publications to the fields of sociology and criminal justice, and have made 41 presentations at professional meetings of sociologists and criminologists. This is my fifth book.

In the second chapter I provide a brief overview of the case for those not familiar with it, or for those who have forgotten about it amidst the deluge of news that has cascaded our way since, May, 2003, when Derrick Lee was apprehended.

In Chapter 3 I point out how a sense of injustice, critical to the formation of any social movement, was slowly building in Baton Rouge as the deaths of several women were linked to the common DNA of an unknown suspect. Then, Chapter 4 documents the strong leadership of Dr. Maurice Godwin, without whose influence the movement would never have jelled into the force that it was, nor would it have had the unique character as a social forum that it had. The citizens of Baton Rouge followed his lead, including family members of the slain women, and the results were truly remarkable. Godwin provided a steady hand of guidance to keep the movement on track and to keep it from becoming a forum of wild speculation about the serial killer, as some other Internet discussion groups related to the case had become.

The death of Carrie Yoder, discussed in Chapter 5, is probably the seminal event of the book and the precipitant of the most intense and important activity, both by the Internet social movement and by the Task Force investigating the serial killer case. The remainder of the book discusses what happened after the arrest of Derrick Lee, the rapid decline of the social movement on the Internet, and the possible reasons why this precipitous decline occurred. The last chapter provides updates and sociological analysis on the case including breaking news on the expected execution date of Derrick Lee. What was the end result of the serial killer case? Are women in Baton Rouge safer now than they were before?

ENDNOTES

1. Susan Mustafa, Tony Clayton, and Sue Israel, *I've Been Watching You: The South Louisiana Serial Killer*. Bloomington: Author House, 2006.

2. Stephanie Stanley, *An Invisible Man*. New York: Berkley Books, 2006.

3. Maurice Godwin, *Tracker: Hunting Down Serial Killers*. New York: Thunder's Mouth Press, 2005.

Chapter 2

The Baton Rouge Serial Murders:
An Overview

Baton Rouge. In the native French, the name means "Red Stick." In 1699, Sieur d'Iberville led an exploration party of 200 French Canadians up the Mississippi River, and in March, they saw a bluff on the east bank with a cypress pole festooned with bloody animal and fish heads. It was a boundary-marker between the hunting territories of two local Houma Indian groups.[1] Settled by French, English and Spanish adventurers, it would eventually grow into the second largest city in Louisiana, and after the evacuation of New Orleans following Hurricane Katrina, it would emerge as Louisiana's largest city.[2]

Known for its Cajun-Creole culture, delectable food, corrupt politicians, toxic chemicals, violent people, and football, Baton Rouge is a place folks seek out to explore in spite of the obvious hazards. To be sure, there is never a dull moment here. In 2002, the D.C. Beltway snipers John Muhammad and Lee Boyd Malvo stopped by, blowing away a Korean shopkeeper before heading off to Alabama and then to the East Coast to spread fear and mayhem there.[3] For the Baton Rouge native Muhammad, it was his farewell tour of the city. Then, three dead women were linked by DNA to a serial killer, the third of four that would stalk women in the town.[4] Officials appeared resolute to find the killer, but would they? History did not provide cause for optimism. In a state where ineptness, bungling, and scandal are a way of life and sinning is the official pastime, Baton Rouge is the capital.[5]

"We do things differently in Louisiana" is how the outspoken writer Louis Cataldie put it.[6] More often than not, it is the slowest, most inefficient and low tech way of getting something done, great for a tourist with an unhurried itinerary, but not much else. And the old school cops in Baton Rouge were like that. Going slow and deliberate was a way of life for them. In the spring of 2003, however, there were people who were fed up with the old way of doing things. Things were happening fast, and forceful, efficient action was needed. In fact, something horrific had just happened to a bright young student at one of the local colleges, Carrie Lynn Yoder.

That spring, Carrie Yoder was a promising Ph.D. candidate in the Department of Biological Sciences at Louisiana State University. She had passed the General Examination (an oral and written exam on all subject material in the field of biology) the previous January, and she had discussed and defended her proposed dissertation research with her committee.[7] All she had to do to finish her doctorate was to work on her dissertation research and then defend the results before her committee. For many doctoral students, this is the "light at the end of the tunnel," and an indicator that, while much hard work is to be done, the worst of the intellectually grueling graduate training is nearing an end. Then, following graduation, she faced a bright future as a research scientist.

Yoder, 26 years old, went missing on March 3, 2003 from her home at 4250 Dodson Avenue in Baton Rouge where she had been forcibly taken sometime between 6 P.M. and midnight. She lived only a few miles from two other women that had turned up missing; and, she lived alone, like a third woman who had disappeared from her home in Lafayette. Lee Stanton, Yoder's boyfriend of three years, reported her missing to police two days after she failed to contact him.[8]

Stanton told police he had last talked to Yoder on March 3, and she told him she was going to the Winn Dixie grocery store on Burbank Drive. They made plans to talk that night or the following day, but when he did not hear from her he began to worry. The next day he went to check on her and noticed that her car was there and the lights were on in the house, but he did not go in.[9]

Two days later, after still no contact, he decided to return to her house and look inside. He noticed that her keys, cellular phone and purse were on the counter and the back door was open. He then realized that something was terribly wrong.[10]

Stanton immediately called the police. Everything in the house appeared normal except for a wall mounted key holder by the front door, which was dangling by one screw as if knocked off its hinges by force. From this, Stanton suggested that there could have been a struggle in that area, but the police did not suspect foul play.[11]

Carrie Yoder's body was found eight days later. She had been strangled and beaten by Derrick Todd Lee, the man who would later be known as the convicted south Louisiana serial killer. Swabs taken during the autopsy yielded a male DNA which matched the DNA found in the murders of the four women missing in Baton Rouge and Lafayette at the time.[12] Bill Platt, Yoder's doctoral professor, was with Yoder's parents when officials called them to relay the news that Carrie's body had been found.[13] Baton Rouge native Louis Cataldie, who happened to be the Coroner of East Baton Rouge Parish at the time, was called to retrieve the body and perform an autopsy.[14]

The beleaguered head of the police Task Force, Baton Rouge Police Chief Pat Englade, remarked on day of the DNA match: "I understand that the fear and anxiety in this community right now is very high, but let me assure you the Task Force is absolutely committed to finding this killer and there is absolutely no doubt in my mind we will be successful."[15]

It would take ten more agonizing weeks of investigating for the special police unit known as the Multi-Agency Homicide Task Force to name Lee, 34, of St. Francisville, Louisiana as the suspect in the murders of Yoder and the four others: Gina Wilson Green, Charlotte Murray Pace, Pam Kinamore, all of Baton Rouge; and Dene Colomb of Lafayette. As of March, 2003, other cases thought to be linked to the serial killer were the slayings of Christine Moore, Lillian Robinson, and Melinda McGhee.[16] Moore was an LSU student the same age as Yoder; Robinson's body was found near the location where Yoder's was found; and McGhee, though living in Alabama, had an abduction pattern very similar to the women abducted and murdered in Baton Rouge.

All the serial killer's victims were mature, accomplished, independent, intellectual women. Green, 41, was strangled to death in her Stanford Avenue home in Baton Rouge. Pace, 23, was stabbed to death in her Sharlo Avenue townhome. Kinamore, 44, was abducted from her Briarwood Estates home in East Baton Rouge, and was discovered with her throat slashed underneath the Whiskey Bay Bridge off Interstate 10. Columb, 23, was found beaten to death in a rural field in Scott, Louisiana, just outside Lafayette.[17]

The Task Force convened informally in 2001, and by late 2002 and early 2003 the results of the Task Force investigation focused on a white male with an intimidating stare who drove a white truck. Information about the kind of shoes he wore was released to the public, along with a psychological profile. A good deal of this early information turned out to be false.[18]

Lee was a black male with short black hair, brown eyes, 6 foot 1 inch, approximately 210 pounds, and a muscular build. His last known residence was 4273 Highway 61 in St. Francisville.[19] Women who had traveled the "river road," or Highway 61 from Baton Rouge to Natchez, Mississippi had come within yards of the dangerous serial murderer.

People throughout the state of Louisiana were shocked at the rash of deaths at the hands of what now obviously appeared to be a single killer. The residents of southern Louisiana, especially women living in and around the LSU campus in Baton Rouge, were gripped by the daily fear that they might be the killer's next victim.[20] Substantial funds were donated by individuals and organizations toward reward monies for information into the arrest and conviction of the serial killer.[21] On March 16, 2003, the friends and family of some of the victims rallied on the steps of the Louisiana state capitol demanding an end to the murders.[22] They had had enough of the senseless loss of life and the overwhelming, gripping fear that swept Baton Rouge every day that the killer was on the loose. Something more had to be done.

A North Carolina criminologist by the name of Dr. Maurice Godwin claimed to have critical evidence concerning the murders. Godwin had constructed a geographic profile containing the places where the victims disappeared and where their bodies were discovered. He found that the crime scenes formed a triangular shaped pattern on a map, which he believed pinpointed the specific geographic area where the killer lived.[23] He was a veteran student of serial killers, having collected data on 107 previous cases that he had looked at in great detail.

Godwin said that he presented his unique findings to Task Force investigators months before Yoder's death, but they showed no interest at all in his discovery. Godwin further claimed he was able to predict where the next murder would take place. His claim carried even more weight when Yoder was abducted within the triangular-shaped pattern revealed by Godwin.[24] Godwin believed that it was within this triangular shaped geographic area on the map that the next attack would occur.

Near the end of March, 2003 the Task Force reported some important new information. At a press conference, it released a statement that the public should no longer focus primarily on the latest sketches of the suspect previously released by investigators (the white male in the pickup truck), but on a person of any race. Moreover, the public should be on the lookout for more than just the white truck, but any vehicle that might seem suspicious.[25] This was reminiscent of the D.C. Beltway Sniper case, where initial police attention was focused, incorrectly, on a white van.[26]

The big break in the case occurred when DNA obtained from Lee on May 5, 2003, matched a DNA sample taken from the body of Carrie Yoder. The Louisiana Attorney General's investigator, Danny Mixon, had heard that Lee was talking about the disappearance of a Zachary, Louisiana woman named Randi Mebruer, who had vanished from her home in April, 1998. After looking at Lee's criminal history, including arrests for stalking, peeping into homes, burglary and attempted murder, Mixon got a court to order a DNA sample from Lee. On that same day, Lee abruptly pulled his two children out of school, saying he was suddenly planning on moving to Los Angeles.[27]

In 2002 the Task Force began using electronic billboards to run ads about the killer. The boards were used to display up to date information about the murders, including the white truck and a composite of the suspect. The number of billboards increased from two to six during 2003, covering the Lafayette and Baton Rouge area.[28]

At the 18 month mark the Task Force started to receive harsh criticism, one of the most vocal critics being criminologist Dr. Robert Keppel, known for the unique approach he used to investigate serial killers such as Ted Bundy and the Green River killer. In February 2003, he listed four major mistakes made by the task force.[29]

First, there was a great possibility that the murderer's name was already in the Task Force's possession but could easily get overlooked in the files, especially with such a flood of information coming in. According to Keppel, police often obtain the name of a killer within the first 30 days of an investigation.[30]

Second, Keppel said that the Task Force should not have revealed the DNA evidence linking the victims, saying that it might hinder the investigation. The killer would simply adjust tactics and might be more careful in selecting future victims and taking care not to leave behind any evidence of the crime.[31]

Third, revealing information about the killer's shoes would probably have the result of the killer simply disposing of them, making the murders more difficult to connect with him if ever caught.[32]

Fourth, the psychological profile released by the Task Force only adds to the information overload in the case and takes away valuable time from the investigation. The most important information in the case was the composite sketch and the information about the truck. Keppel's offer to help the Task Force was refused.[33]

Of all the criticism received, that of Maurice Godwin would turn out to be among the most significant. A *FOX News* consultant early in the case, his findings were at variance with those of the Task Force, and his information may have placed the greatest amount of pressure on the Task Force investigators to produce results. From his home in Fayetteville, North Carolina, he began a *Yahoo!* discussion group in January, 2003 concerned with the Baton Rouge serial murders. Though he rarely visited Baton Rouge, he was a key player in the Baton Rouge drama by virtue of his careful cataloging and analysis of the Baton Rouge cases using new computer technology and geographic mapping capabilities. The innovative Internet social movement that he created turned out to be a useful hub of information in the efforts to pressure the Task Force for new and improved results.[34] The Internet group consisted mostly of people from Baton Rouge that had become consumed by the case, although Godwin allowed others from further away to join if there was a legitimate personal or professional interest in following the latest developments. It is ultimately up to the reader to determine how much of an influence Godwin's social movement turned out to be, as the Task Force claimed it to be but an annoyance and hindrance in their quest for the truth. But the fact is that the Task Force released Derrick Lee's name to the public on the very day that Dr. Godwin was coming to Baton Rouge to confront the Task Force with new information that he had discovered about the case.

This book is about Godwin's Internet social movement, the one that sprang to life when citizens in Baton Rouge, south Louisiana and south Mississippi grew increasingly upset by the slow pace and lack of progress of the multi-jurisdictional Task Force seeking the Baton Rouge serial killer. I am an insider to this movement, having participated and observed it since it first appeared on the Internet beginning in January of 2003.[35] I describe and analyze sociologically the key players, the major controversies and the internal dynamics of the movement that kept the heat on the multi-unit Task Force up until the arrest of Derrick Todd Lee on May 27, 2003. Pat Englade and others on the Task Force downplayed the work of Godwin, but the big news in the case, the arrest of Derrick Lee, came just as Godwin's internet social movement had ratcheted up pressure on the Task Force almost to the breaking point.[36]

I will discuss in a sociological sense how this movement was driven by the powerful media images of its involvement in the case, and how people are transformed by their participation in the movement. This "media hunger" was among the more negative aspects of the Internet social movement. Once the killer had been identified, and the media was no longer interested in the critical question of the identity of the suspect, the social movement essentially vanished into thin air.[37] That may seem odd considering how hard the movement participants pressed the investigators; yet, we will see that this is fairly typical of social movements in an image-driven, media conscious world.

Scholars contend that social movements in our current "postmodern" world are much different from ones in earlier eras. Sixties era social movements had "us versus them" qualities, and the points of dispute were critical, long lasting issues such as the Vietnam War. Today, movements tend to be ad-hoc affairs, arising over local issues. They are often temporary: once the social problem has been solved, the movement disappears. They involve what is called "cross over participation" from people in parallel or closely related movements. And they are often highly technological movements that are media driven, the powerful media images of the social movement in progress are often more important than what the movement itself actually accomplishes.[38]

All four conditions apply to the Baton Rouge serial killer case. The movement arose on the Internet specifically to address the missing women in Baton Rouge and the efforts of the Task Force to solve the case. At its peak, it was a sort of private task force that was an improvised tool to pool resources and to get to the bottom of the case. Second, the movement in Baton Rouge was indeed temporary, it essentially fell apart after Lee's arrest and though nominally still alive, barely functioned at all during 2005 and 2006, and in 2007 lies dormant. Third, women's advocates and self defense experts, among others, used the serial killer case to promote their products and to educate women on how to avoid being made into a victim by the likes of Lee. Thus, they "crossed over" to join the Internet movement. And fourth, movement participants basked in the limelight of the media attention they received, and this encouraged them to persist in applying public pressure to the Task Force. As neophyte Columbos they awkwardly pressed forward in hopes of finding the identity of the killer and bringing him to justice.

We know, also, that unique features of the Internet render any social movement formed there distinctively different from the kinds that preceded it before the Internet was born. Sociologists have written about how involvement in Internet social groups can lead to a neglect of traditional face to face family and friends and the replacement of these by "electronic primary groups" that replace the key face to face family bonds with those of electronic friends.[39] We have reason to believe that this happened more than once in the serial killer case, as some became prolific or even exhaustive posters to the Internet discussion group, and only later found it prudent to take a much needed break to recover from the intense work and emotional labor surrounding the discussion group. One woman posted over 400 messages in the period from January through June, 2003 when interest in the case was at its peak.[40]

It occurred to me that the story of this fledgling, yet powerful, social movement on the Internet may never be written unless someone takes the time to do it now. The Internet, while a popular phenomenon, is also a fickle one. The initial discussion group that gave birth to the citizens' movement is still alive, but basically has been on life support ever since the arrest of Derrick Todd Lee. Should *Yahoo!* decide that traffic on the group is too low, or if Dr. Godwin chooses at any time to resign as the group's moderator, there's a distinct possibility that all the discussions in the group's archive will be lost forever unless someone steps forward to take Dr. Godwin's place as moderator. In my opinion, the time to capture a history of the movement is right now.

Social movement organizing on the Internet will be the wave of the future. The Internet movement analyzed in this book is truly a model of how it can be done and done well. Even if you come away from the book with negative attitudes about what the social movement in the serial killer case claimed to accomplish, the history of the movement will be empowering to others who have identified an important social problem and want to solve it, and who are seeking a model of how problems can be solved using Internet participants. For open minded police administrators, such groups could even be embraced as partners in crime fighting in unusual cases such as that in Baton Rouge.

Upon word of being sought by officials in Baton Rouge, Derrick Lee tried to escape, first to Chicago and then to Atlanta, where U.S. Marshals captured him. He was eventually convicted for the murders of Charlotte Pace and Geralyn De-Soto, with the DNA evidence providing substantial proof of guilt.[41] In January, 2005, prosecutors in Lafayette, the hometown of Dene Colomb, declined to prosecute Lee, citing the two convictions and Lee's current residence on death row at the State Prison at Angola, Louisiana. They will proceed only if Lee's death penalty convictions are overturned.[42]

As of early September, 2005, Lee's attorneys were pursuing an appeal of Lee's convictions to the Louisiana Supreme Court. Lee's brief before the court was due September 8, while the state's brief was due October 8.[43] The devastation wrought by hurricanes Katrina and Rita forced the closure of the Supreme Court for several weeks, delaying progress in the Lee case.[44] In 2006, a woman who survived an attack by Lee sued Crime Stoppers for the $150,000 reward for information leading to his arrest and conviction. Crime Stoppers insisted that victims of Lee's attacks could not receive any of the money.[45]

In pursing their appeal, Lee's attorneys contended that the Charlotte Pace trial should have been moved from Baton Rouge because many prospective jurors were aware that Lee was convicted in nearby Port Allen, Louisiana in August, 2004 for killing Geralyn DeSoto, yet another victim linked to Lee. Many prospective jurors said before the Pace trial began that Lee was guilty. The lawyers also claim Lee is mentally retarded, and that evidence from other murders Lee is accused of committing should not have been presented to jurors.[46]

The broader implications of the serial killer case were felt soon after Lee was arrested and will probably continue to echo on for years. Pat Englade, chair of the multi-unit Task Force, resigned as Police Chief of Baton Rouge in September, 2004, only a few months after the arrest of Derrick Lee. Then, in November, 2004, Mayor Bobby Simpson was defeated in his bid to be reelected as Mayor of Baton Rouge.[47] Some felt that Englade's resignation came too late to help Simpson in his reelection bid. And the heat is now on the new Mayor and Police Chief to do all they can to make sure the women of Baton Rouge are safe. There is still a residue of pain and dissatisfaction, and a serious public perception that not enough had been done to solve the serial killer case. More citizen input, including the use of alternative criminological experts, might have saved the lives of several women who fell pray to the serial killer, especially Carrie Yoder, who paid the ultimate price for the slow pace of the Task Force.

ENDNOTES

1. Rose Meyers, *A History of Baton Rouge, 1699-1812*. Baton Rouge: Louisiana State University Press, 1976.

2. Meyers, *ibid*; Wil Haygood, "After Katrina, Baton Rouge Weathers a Storm of Its Own," *Washington Post*, August 25, 2006.

3. Louis Cataldie, *Coroner's Journal*. New York: G.P. Putnam's Sons, 2005; Stan Weeber, "Targeted Violence, Collective Behavior and Criminology: The D.C. Beltway Sniper Case," *Virginia Social Science Journal*, Volume 40, Winter, 2005: 1-17.

4. Cataldie, *ibid*.

5. Baton Rouge: Scandal on the Bayou," *City Confidential*, Episode 53, Season 5, aired August 2, 2003; Ann Brewster Dobie, *Wide Awake in the Pelican State*. Baton Rouge: Louisiana State University Press, 2006; Marcia Gaudet and James C. McDonald (Eds.) *Mardi Gras, Gumbo, and Zydeco*. Jackson: University Press of Mississippi, 2003.

6. Cataldie, *ibid*.

7. "In Carrie's Memory," Department of Biological Sciences, Louisiana State University. Available online at: http://www.lsu.edu/findcarrie/ (accessed June, 1, 2005).

8. "The Mystery of the Baton Rouge Serial Killer," *Crime Library*. Available online at: http://www.crimelibrary.com (accessed June 1, 2005).

9. *Ibid.*

10. *Ibid.*

11. *Ibid.*

12. *Ibid.*

13. Josh Noel and Emily Kern, "Professor Says Family 'Very Certain' It's Yoder," *Baton Rouge Advocate*, March 14, 2003.

14. Cataldie, *ibid.*

15. "DNA Evidence Links Murder of Carrie Lynn Yoder to the Serial Killer," *Baton Rouge Advocate*, March 18, 2003.

16. "Derrick Todd Lee," *Crime Library*, accessed September 15, 2005.

17. *Ibid.*

18. Josh Noel, "Police Statement on Lee Contradicts Early Reports," *Baton Rouge Advocate*, November 13, 2003.

19. Press Release, Multi Agency Homicide Task Force, May 26, 2003.

20. "Hunting Evil," *Crime Library*, accessed September 15, 2005.

21. *Ibid.*

22 *Ibid.*

23. *Ibid.*

24. *Ibid.*

25. *Ibid.*

26. Michael Shnayerson, "The Net's Master Data-Miner," *Vanity Fair.Com*. Available online at http://www.vanityfair.com (accessed September 5, 2006).

27. Kari Sable Burns, "The Politics of Murder: Will Baton Rouge Clean House?" Available online at: http://www.karisable.com/skazbr3.htm (accessed September 3, 2005).

28. "Baton Rouge Billboards Urge Vigilance," *WDSU News*, March 26, 2003.

29. "Hunting Evil," *ibid.*

30. *Ibid.*

31. *Ibid.*

32. *Ibid.*

33. *Ibid.*

34. *Ibid.*

35. I joined this group in late January, 2003, just a few days after it was initiated by Maurice Godwin.

36. "Hunting Evil," *ibid.*

37. See discussion in Chapter 6.

38. See Michael Moore and Lynda Moore, "Fall from Grace: Implications of the O.J. Simpson Trial for Postmodern Criminal Justice," *Sociological Spectrum*, 17, 1997: 305-322.

39. James Henslin, *Essentials of Sociology.* Boston: Allyn and Bacon, 2005: 115.

40. From the archive of the discussion group.

41. "Second Murder Trial," *Crime Library*, accessed September 5, 2005.

42. "Record of Derrick Todd Lee Trial Given to Supreme Court," *KATC News*, accessed September 3, 2005.

43. Joe Gyan, "Lee's Supreme Court Appeal Gets Number, Brief Deadlines," *Baton Rouge Advocate*, August 23, 2005.

44. Robert Gunn, "Louisiana Supreme Court Closure," September 29, 2005.

45. Gyan, *ibid.*

46. *Ibid.*

47. Rachel Flarity, "Students Await Holden's Changes," *The Daily Reveille*, Louisiana State University, November 23, 2004.

Chapter 3

A Sense of Injustice Builds

Academic sociology as well as a good dose of common sense tells us that many social movements arise from local issues and problems which remain unsolved and around which a sense of injustice builds. A key moment in the rise of the civil rights movement, for example, was the refusal of Rosa Parks to give up her seat to a white man on a Birmingham, Alabama city bus.[1] More recently, local issues have been important in such diverse movements as the movement to house the homeless in Atlanta, the use of "protest art" in authoritarian contexts, and the female inheritance movement in Hong Kong.[2] Given this emphasis on locality, one would suspect that the local social movement that sought the identity of the Baton Rouge serial killer would have been headed or influenced by a local person, but that was not the case. Strangely enough, a North Carolinian was in charge of the movement.

Part of this peculiarity had to do with the new medium of the Internet. The Internet is transforming our sense of what "local" means. It is possible with substantial effort to have the feeling of living and working in a particular place while being far away. Through innovations such as telecommuting and distance learning, workers and students alike no longer have to be tied to a given time or place in order to fulfill their requirements.[3] Maurice Godwin extended this model to the science of tracking criminals as he stalked the Baton Rouge serial killer from 900 miles away in Fayetteville, North Carolina.

Apparently making use of the "breaking news" functions of the local news outlets or at least carefully and constantly monitoring them, Godwin seemed to know what was going on in Baton Rouge before most of the locals did. And because he made his living through geographic mapping, he was a quick study when it came to maps, and was probably more familiar with the geography of Louisiana's capital city than most of the locals were. Thus, a native North Carolinian who rarely set foot in Baton Rouge became the top alternative expert seeking the Baton Rouge serial killer.

Dr. Godwin received his Associate's degree from Vance-Granville Community College in North Carolina, a Bachelor's degree from Trevecca Nazarene University in Nashville, a Master's Degree from Indiana State University, and his doctorate in investigative psychology from The University of Liverpool in England. He now teaches at East Carolina University in Greenville, North Carolina. In the spring of 2003 he taught at Methodist College in Fayetteville, North Carolina and performed his research there.[4]

Godwin's company, Godwin Trial & Forensic Consultancy is a multidisciplinary company whose services include helping defense attorneys detect errors made by crime scene investigators, and assisting attorneys in developing trial strategies that will diminish the testimony of the opposition's profiling expert.[5]

Godwin is a former police officer in the state of North Carolina. He was one of the first project coordinators for a National Institute of Justice grant for implementing community policing in a rural area. Dr. Godwin is also the author of numerous books and journal articles on psychological, serial murder, and geographical profiling. He has worked as a consultant to police and others in developing psychological and geographical profiles. He has lectured in the United States and Europe on serial murder, cyber stalking, and criminal investigative analysis.[6]

Dr. Godwin is best known as the criminal and geographical profiler who has accurately profiled the Washington, D.C. sniper case plus many more serial cases. He has appeared on numerous national TV shows such as *Hardball, Connie Chung, Fox News Live, MSNBC, CNN,* and *Geraldo Rivera.* His expertise and scientific research in areas of psychology, criminal behavior, and criminology distinctly sets him apart from the vast number of forensic, clinical, and psychological consultants who rely on intuitive based opinions.[7]

Because of Godwin's record of scholarly publications, Baton Rouge Chief of Police Pat Englade accused Godwin of using the Baton Rouge case as a means to collect to collect more data to write yet another book. He tried to paint him as an exploiter of a difficult situation. Godwin bristled at the suggestion.[8] Ironically, Englade later floated the idea of using his own experience in the case as the basis for writing his own book.[9] Godwin, however, did write two book chapters related to the Baton Rouge case.[10]

Because of his background and training, Maurice Godwin felt comfortable, even confident leading a social movement in a place he'd hardly spent any time in. In many ways, it was just another case to solve, this time with a twist: he would lead a social movement on the Internet, and he would use some of the people in the movement as his eyes and ears, his "boots on the ground" so to speak, to observe things that he could not. Thus equipped, his social movement on the Internet was born in mid-January of 2003. He suspected that a serial killer was on the loose long before then, however.

Godwin believed that there was a serial killer stalking women in Baton Rouge long before anyone else because of the geographic tracking technique that he uses. That technique connects cases that otherwise might be considered unrelated; such was the case with two of the earliest Baton Rouge victims since 2001, Gina Green and Charlotte Murray Pace. Green and Pace had been neighbors and thus were connected to a specific geographic area. This was important as Dr. Godwin suspected early on that whoever the killer was, he was a "viper," or one that lays low and attacks in the same area.[11] They typically don't venture out very far to attack and dump their victims. That being the case, the geographic link between the two women was significant. Pace had lived just three doors down from the town homes where Green lived, and Pace had just moved to another apartment at 1211 Sharlo Avenue, where she was killed.[12] The killer followed her there and killed her as a target of convenience. While the police could find little to link the two crimes, Godwin could feel the wind of the red flags churning in his office.

Godwin's profiling method comes in a package called Predator, and it is actually a complex mix of both quantitative and qualitative scientific methods. Also called Psycho-Geographic Profiling, it is concerned with the spatial analysis and psychological behavioral patterns of criminals. The technique employs a variety of methods, including distance to crime research, demographic analysis, environmental psychology, landscape analysis, geographic information systems, point pattern analysis, crime site residual analysis, and psychological criminal profiling. This technique is a particularly effective method for the needs of police investigators attempting to solve complex serial crimes such as the Baton Rouge case. It examines the spatial data connected to a series of crime sites as well as victims' body dump sites and point of fatal encounter sites.[13]

The landscape analysis is the qualitative tool used. In this phase of the analysis, geo-forensic analysis attempts to reconstruct the course of travel of the killer and the victim from before the crime until well after it. Every reasonable effort is made to lay down a complete trail for each person in the crime.[14]

The ultimate goal of Predator is prediction of where the offender will strike next, and as such can provide a measure of advance time to gear up for avoiding the killer and to plan various means of fighting back. Being able to predict where the killer will strike next is the ultimate selling point for Predator as it specifies an area that police can search immediately for clues.[15]

But Dr. Godwin is quick to point out that the psycho-geographic profiling all by itself does not actually solve crimes.[16] It provides an additional avenue of scientific investigation that, with the many other forensic specialties, may provide some help for the investigation of a serial killing. It can provide an additional perspective that may assist police during the investigation of a serial murder in which bodies of victims are scattered over a large geographic area. The method seems also to be able to indicate that a sequence of murders belongs in one serial, even when the police deny such an interpretation.[17] The method successfully predicted the social characteristics and the geographic distribution of the serial murders committed by John Williams, Jr. in Raleigh, North Carolina, and it predicted where William Reece lived, Reece being the killer of Laura Smither of Friendswood, Texas.[18]

A typical prediction area is wedge-shaped, resembling a piece of pie. Analyses have shown that there is an 80 percent probability that the criminal lives or works within that wedge. This is the area in which police should search for the perpetrator.[19]

The death of Pam Kinamore only confirmed Godwin's worse fears about the situation in Baton Rouge. More forceful and more carefully directed investigation was badly needed. He had information that would have helped investigators, but his information was not taken seriously by the Task Force investigating the serial killer case, at least not at first.

Kinamore was abducted from her Baton Rouge home July 12, 2002. She was last seen at her antique shop in Denham Springs that night. Authorities found her car in her driveway, with her keys left in the door. The 44-year old mother and wife had recently drawn a bath. Her throat was slit and her body dumped about 30 miles away from Baton Rouge, near Whiskey Bay off of Interstate 10.

Pam's murder was under the jurisdiction of the coroner and sheriff in Iberville Parish, but her body eventually made its way back to the LSU forensics lab where Louis Cataldie was once again called upon to do a forensics examination. Not taking any chances, he put the body through a full body X-ray to see if there were any clues, such as bone fractures that might indicate a certain type of trauma, or nicks on her ribs that might indicate stab wounds.[20] This was necessary as the remains were badly decomposed. He also sent the body to be X-rayed at a special lab called FACES at LSU because he was looking for a skull fracture that might indicate an attack to her head. Then, he returned her to the parish morgue for a second autopsy and review by Dr. Michael Cramer. Cataldie knew too well how botched forensics exams and autopsies had corrupted the evidence in a number of other cases, and proceeded with an abundance of caution.[21]

Kinamore's mother, Lynne Marino, was quite frankly upset with how disinterested the police were in tracking Pam's killer, even though there was a serial killer on the loose targeting attractive professional women. She found no bloodhounds sniffing the trail, no army of police searching for the killer in the nearby woods, no helicopters and no planes with heat-sensing detectors dispatched. No one from the FBI showed up, nor was there a wiretap of Pam's phone in anticipation of a phone in anticipation of a ransom call.[22] The TV version of missing person's cases bore no resemblance to the real life nightmare Ms. Marino was living out in Baton Rouge. The cops even put Pam's wheel-chair bound husband Byron under suspicion, much to Cataldie's chagrin.[23]

When an FBI partial profile of the killer was released, Godwin was very critical of the way the bureau was handling the evidence and communicating it to the public, and he had several issues with matters related to Kinamore's death. The following are portions of the FBI's profile along with Godwin's comments:

FBI: This offender did not want, nor did he expect for Pam Kinamore's body to be found. On Tuesday, July 16, 2002, when it was announced that her body was found near the Whiskey Bay Exit off of Interstate 10, he would have been noticeably upset, agitated, angry and preoccupied. Those around him may recall his having made comments that there was no way the Kinamore murder was connected to the other two.

Godwin: The above statement is stating the obvious. It is blatantly clear, that the killer disposed of Ms. Kinamore's body in a remote location in order to destroy any physical evidence such as DNA. Also, this fact suggests that the killer follows the news reports about the murders.

FBI: This offender may have even returned to the Whiskey Bay area, to the scene where he left Kinamore's body, because he was so perplexed about her having been found. This return to that area may have appeared to have been for "legitimate" reasons, for example he was "curious" about what the area looked like.

Godwin: I seriously doubt that the killer returned to the location where Ms. Kinamore's body was discovered. The notion that the killer was 'curious' about what the area looked like is ludicrous. I suggest that due to public and police pressure that the killer stayed a good distance from Ms. Kinamore's body discovery site.

FBI: This offender has followed this investigation in the media. His attention to the media reports would be inconsistent with his prior behavior about current events in Baton Rouge, in which he displayed little interest. On Friday July 12, 2002, two days after the announcement the Pace and Green murders were connected by DNA, Pam Kinamore is taken out of her home. It is likely this change in his MO is a direct result of his having learned about the Pace-Green connection through the media.

Godwin: Oh, really!! I would have never guessed this!! Please!![24]

Kinamore's death dramatically escalated the level of fear in the city. The apparent randomness of the killer's choice of victims meant that any woman in the city could be the next victim, especially those that are upwardly mobile professional women. A woman told *CBS News*: "If I have to resort to buying a gun, I will and that's what I'm doing."[25] She was by no means alone in her fear. Self-defense classes were filling up fast with frightened women. Even the state's top public official was alarmed: "Get mace, carry a baseball bat, lock your doors, don't let anybody in you don't know," said Louisiana Governor Mike Foster.[26]

On the Louisiana State University campus near the scene of two of the murders, joggers paired up for their own safety. Worried parents were taking students home. "If any parents are concerned about their child they should call the school or keep their children home until this is solved," Lynne Marino told *CBS*.[27]

Fear also was the apparent driving force behind a number of rumors about the serial killer that all turned out to be untrue, rumors that sociologists later called "urban legends" because of the persistent way in which the stories circulated and continued to circulate despite the constant assurances of the police and other public officials that there was nothing of substance to any of the rumors. Here is what appears to be the text of an original rumor that was copied frequently on the Internet:

> Hi friends and family. I know that with all the psychos out there, we still think that something couldn't really happen to us, right? Wrong! As most of you know, I live in Alexandria, but I work in Lafayette where I stay with friends when I'm there.

> As you know from *America's Most Wanted* TV program as well as the news media, there is a serial killer in the Lafayette area. I just want to let you know about an "incident" that happened to me a few weeks ago that could have been deadly.

> At first I didn't go to the police or anyone with it because I didn't realize how serious this encounter was. But since I work in a jail and I told a few people about it, it wasn't long before I was paraded into Internal Affairs to tell them my story.

> It was approximately 5:15 am in Opelousas, La. I had stayed with a friend there and I was on my way to work. I stopped at the Exxon/Blimpie station to get gas. I got $10 gas and a Diet Coke...I took into the store two $5 bills and one $1 bill. (just enough to get my stuff)

> As I pulled away from the store, a man approached my truck from the back side of the store (an unlit area). He was an "approachable-looking" man (clean cut, clean shaven, dressed well, etc). He walked up to my window and knocked. Since I'm very paranoid and "always looking for the rapist or killer", I didn't open the window....I just asked what he wanted. He raised a $5 bill to my window and said "You dropped this."

Since I knew I had gone into the store with a certain amount of money....I knew I didn't drop it. When I told him it wasn't mine....he began hitting the window and door and screaming at me to open my door and that I had dropped the money! At that point, I drove away as fast as I could.

After talking to the Internal Affairs department and describing the man I saw and the way he escalated from calm and polite to angry and volatile...it was determined that I could have possibly encountered the serial killer myself. At this point, it is unclear as to how he gains access to his victims since there has been no evidence of forced entry into homes, etc. And the fact that he has been attacking in the daytime when women are less likely to have their guard up...and what gesture is nicer than returning money to someone that dropped it????? How many times would you have opened your window (or door) to get your money and say thank you....because if the person is kind enough to return something to you...then he can't really be a threat....can he????

Please be cautious! This might not have been the serial killer....it probably wasn't.... but anyone that gets that angry over someone not accepting money from them, can't have honorable intentions.[28]

In variations of the story that appeared on the Internet, most of the text remains the same although the location changes frequently. That is, instead of the incident happening in Opelousas, it happens in Flint, Michigan or Tallahassee, Florida or Berea, Ohio.[29]

There also appeared to be a series of similarly frightening stories that were spun off of this one, or were circulated with the same urgency as the one above. Here is one example:

Hello friends-

I am writing to tell you all about an incident that happened tonight (Sunday) at the Wal-Mart here in New Iberia. This is not a chain letter or urban legend as it really happened to me just a little while a go. Like an idiot, I went to Wal-Mart at 7:30 at night. While I was in the candy aisle, getting Valentine candy for my Godchildren, a white guy started talking to me. He was looking at candy just like I was so I didn't notice him at first. Anyway, he began to ask me questions about my shoes, were they comfortable, did they give me blisters, how did I keep them on my feet, etc. Just chatting. (I was wearing my "nun shoes"; Brown leather slip on shoes) They are very comfortable but not very, trust me. Well he was already kneeling down to look at candy and as he was talking to me, he reached over and touched my shoe and then moved his hand around to the back of my shoe and brushed my skin. Lightbulb moment: this is not normal. I don't let strangers touch my feet unless I am paying them for a pedicure.

I moved away quickly and as I was moving, he asked if I would help him pick some out like mine for his sister. Another lightbulb. I told him no and got away as quickly as I could. During my shopping trip, I asked an employee to have someone walk me out. (The guy came walking up behind us as we talked and he turned off quickly when he saw me talking to an employee.)

When I told her the story, she called a manager. When I told her what happened, she asked me to talk to the police who happened to be there for another reason. She told me that they have had several complaints at the Abbeville store of a man doing the same thing, following the women in the store, and then following them home. The policeman walked me out. The guy had short hair, a goatee, an earring in his bottom lip (a stud below the lip), wore a greenish/gray polar fleece pullover with baggy jeans.

I am not sending this to scare you but to let you know to be aware. As paranoid as I have been about the serial killer stuff, I was a prime target tonight. Gullible, easy, trusting. Be careful. Send this to women you know.[30]

The police in several parts of south Louisiana were also spending a good bit of time stamping out rumors that had suddenly erupted like a prairie fire in their towns, often with multiple sightings of the same fictitious event, as the following news coverage suggests in a New Orleans newspaper:

Mandeville police had more than 40 calls in one recent day about a woman having nearly been kidnapped from outside a store in Mandeville's biggest shopping center. At least half of the callers said they heard the would-be kidnapper was driving a white pickup truck, as did the Baton Rouge serial killer.

It never happened. There wasn't even a shoplifter at the store that day, nothing that would have caused police cars to converge and give rise to curiosity and unfounded rumors, Mandeville Police Chief Tom Buell said afterward. "I don't know what started it," Buell said.

Stories came out of Covington this week about a woman who was walking through her neighborhood being followed by a man in a white pickup truck. Later in the week, there was talk of something that might have occurred at another big store between Covington and Mandeville and other reports that the FBI was swarming around the Mandeville area, preparing to arrest the serial killer.

"Even as late as yesterday," Buell said Friday, "my wife came home with another story she about something that was supposed to have occurred. There are a lot of rumors out there."[31]

And another case involved a situation in Metairie involving a white truck:

An article appeared in the Saturday, February 1, 2003 edition of the *Times Picayune* titled "Truck probe called dead end." I cannot retrieve it thru archives and I cannot get an email copy from the author, but I did keep the article. So, here goes an excerpt:

A woman told police that on January 20, a man driving a white pickup truck stopped in front of her house as she worked in her yard in the Palm Vista area of Kenner, near the Metairie line. (This is right on Lake Ponchartrain, with easy access to I-10.) The man asked her some questions about her garden but never got out of the truck...."He was just staring at her with a kind of harassing smirk on his face. He asked her about a plant or a bush in her garden then started to drive off and stopped again and looked at her," Caraway said (Capt. Steve Caraway is the Kenner police spokesman.)...The woman became uncomfortable and went inside, but she didn't call the police right away. It wasn't until January 24 when the woman noticed a resemblance between the man and a sketch of "a person of interest" in the Baton Rouge serial killer case, that she decided to call the police to report the incident.

Now a summary of the rest of the article...Detectives forwarded the information to investigators working on the Baton Rouge serial killer case, but no connection was made, thus the title of the article, "Truck probe called dead end."

This incident happened on Monday, January 20, which was MLK Day, a holiday.[32]

Similar rumors swept Louisiana towns after Hurricane Katrina. Then, the rumors were about Katrina evacuees that were supposedly robbing businesses at gunpoint, raping local women, rioting in the streets and hijacking locals' cars.[33] These reports were mostly untrue.

In the midst of such chaos and fear in 2003, police were urging calm. They did not want the public to panic, but at the same time, they also wanted people to be aware that there is someone out there killing women. A white Chevy pickup, the one mentioned in the above e-mails, was one of the few leads that police would talk about early on. They chose to not release much information as it would essentially be briefing the killer on what the authorities knew about him.[34]

Kinamore's family had made her death a high profile crusade in a city where 30 other unsolved murder cases over the last decade were being re-opened. This was the beginning of a social movement in which a sense of injustice is shared by participants. People began to gather in public for prayer vigils which drew not only those who knew Kinamore or one of the other victims, but by those women that were living in fear as the serial killer roamed loose.[35] "Where will he strike next?" "You know he hasn't established a definite pattern so everybody needs to be aware," according to Lynne Marino.[36] At least this was a concerned layman's view of things; Dr. Godwin had other ideas.

The press began to be interested in the burgeoning social movement after July 22, 2002, when DNA testing confirmed that the three homicides, Pace, Green and Kinamore, were the work of the same killer. Suddenly, all the journalists who had initially ignored the distraught families and friends began returning their calls. Three days after the three murders were linked, Baton Rouge Mayor Bobby Simpson and other top state and local public officials held a press conference in a show of public support for the police. Additional pressure for action came from the mother of one of the deceased victims. On August 1 Lynne Marino called Governor Mike Foster's live radio show and asked him to intervene. After this request, the governor directed the State Police to assist with the probe, which was already in motion. "The agencies just came together because of the urgency of the situation," said Baton Rouge Police Corporal Mary Ann Godawa. In fact, that same day, the Task Force established its headquarters in the Office of Emergency Preparedness building near the Baton Rouge airport. Briefings on the case began on August 5.[37] The press coverage, in turn, helped to add fuel to a generalized public interest in the case well beyond the few victims' relatives that had been the strongest participants in the movement up to that point. The press briefings by Godawa were daily at first but became less frequent later as there was little or no news to report in the investigation.[38]

Behind closed doors at police headquarters, investigators were feeling the heat of public pressure. They were desperate for clues, any clues, and they were exploring connections that might link the three dead women. As of August, 2002, they had found the following common similarities and differences between victims:

- Pace and Green both drove BMWs.

- Pace and Green both jogged on the same lakeside path near LSU.

- Green and Kinamore both had an interest in antiques. Pace, however, liked everything to be an hour and half old and shiny," according to her mother, Ann Pace.

- Green and Kinamore share some physical characteristics and were both older, petite women. Pace was tall and young.

- All three were brunettes.

- There was no forced entry in any of the victims' homes.[39]

Before long, there was a fourth victim to consider in the mix of data being sorted out. As her case was different in many ways from the others, a reorientation in thinking about the serial killer was necessary.

Dene Colomb was a 23-year old future Marine Corps recruit. She was the fourth woman to die in 17 months at the hands of the serial killer, and was the only victim living outside of the Baton Rouge area. She lived at 203 Diamond Drive, Lafayette, Louisiana. She was reported missing on Thursday afternoon, November 21, 2002. Two days after she was reported missing, a hunter found her body in a wooded area in the southern Louisiana town of Scott, just west of Lafayette. That was about 20 miles from where her abandoned car was discovered, in Grand Coteau on a rural road. Her body was recovered on Sunday, November 24. The cause of death was blunt trauma to the head. The killer had crossed over the mythical racial barrier that serial killers are not supposed to cross.[40] Fear escalated even more as the serial killer appeared to have the ability to strike at will and the police and public were helpless to defend themselves. Worse still, the killer was learning as he went along, and was now actively trying to outwit his pursuers. Meanwhile, an eager group on the Internet awaited Dr. Godwin's entry into the case.

In January, 2003, the Task Force announced "a major development" in the case, releasing pictures of a pair of athletic shoes the killer could have been wearing during one of the homicides. It appealed to members of the public for clues. "We don't think he's going to turn himself in, but we think someone who knows him may provide that call ... identifying who this individual is," said Lafayette Parish Sheriff Mike Neustrom.[41] The purpose at this point was to prevent further acts of violence.

A shoe print matching a $40 pair of "Adidas-type" basketball shoes that can be purchased in a number of stores around Lafayette and Baton Rouge was found November 24 "in the immediate vicinity" of where the body of Trineisha (Dene) Colomb was found, Neustrom said.[42] "This information is designed to get someone who is an acquaintance, a friend, an ex-wife, a roommate of the individual who was wearing this type of shoe around November 21st, 22nd, 23rd" to notify authorities about their suspicions."[43]

An FBI psychiatric profile of the killer describes him as an impulsive, aggressive risk-taker who lives between Lafayette and Baton Rouge, knows the area well, and lives a "fairly normal life."[44] His finances were thought to be limited, however, and this was thought to limit his activities to a relatively specific geographic area.

In December, 2002, authorities had begun to open up more to the public with information that they held regarding possible suspects. They said they were searching for a "person of interest" who was spotted in a white pickup truck about 500 feet from where the latest victim was found. Police have said they are searching for a white early 1990s Chevrolet or GMC pickup truck with a fish sticker on the tailgate, with chrome bumpers. That truck was seen near where Colomb's vehicle was abandoned in Grand Coteau. A truck of similar description was reported where Kinamore's body was found.[45]

A man deemed suspicious was reportedly seen November 21, the day before Colomb was reported missing - in a rural, wooded area of Scott. Neustrom said the man was seated in a white early 1990s pickup, with chrome front and rear bumpers - about 500 feet from where Colomb's body was found. As of January 23, 2003, a tip line had received more than 11,700 calls.[46] The public was getting more involved now as just about everyone knew someone who fit the profile released by the Task Force, and they were not at all shy about sharing these possible suspects with those who manned the tip line.

ENDNOTES

1. Douglas Brinkley, *Rosa Parks*. New York: Viking, 2000.

2. Ken Tucci and Jan Worthington, *The Mad Housers: Shelters for the Homeless*. Princeton: Films for the Humanities and Science, 1990; Jacqueline Adams, "When Art Loses its Sting: The Evolution of Protest Art in Authoritarian Contexts," *Sociological Perspectives*, 48, 4, Winter, 2005, pp. 531-558; Inoue Masamichi, "The Female Inheritance Movement in Hong Kong," *Current Anthropology*, 46, 3, June, 2005, p. 403.

3. Paul Jackson and Jos van der Wielen, *Teleworking International Perspectives: From Telecommuting to the Virtual Organization*. New York: Routledge, 2002.

4. This information appears on the professional web page of Dr. Maurice Godwin at: www.investigativepsych.com.

5. *Ibid.*

6. *Ibid.*

7. *Ibid.*

8. Posted to the discussion group May 28, 2003.

9. Posted November 6, 2003.

10. Maurice Godwin, *Tracker: Hunting Down Serial Killers*. New York: Thunder's Mouth Press, 2005.

11. *Ibid.*

12. *Ibid.*

13. This information appears on the professional web page of Dr. Maurice Godwin at: www.investigativepsych.com.

14. *Ibid.*

15. *Ibid.*

16. *Ibid.*

17. *Ibid.*

18. *Ibid.*

19. Maurice Godwin, *Tracker*, p. 10.

20. Cataldie, *ibid.*

21. *Ibid*; Cyril Wecht and Mark Curriden, *Tales From The Morgue*. Amherst, NY: Prometheus Books, 2005; Jarrett Hallcox, *Bodies We've Buried*. New York: Berkley Books, 2006; Michael Baden, *Unnatural Death*. New York: Random House, 1989; Frederick Zugibe, *Dissecting Death*. New York: Broadway Books, 2005.

22. Stephanie Stanley, *An Invisible Man*. New York: Berkley Books, 2006.

23. Cataldie, *ibid.*

24. From www.investigativepsych.com

25. *CBS Evening News*, "A City Gripped by Fear," August 7, 2002.

26. *Ibid.*

27. *Ibid.*

28. http://www.snopes.com/crime/warnings/batonrouge.asp

29. *Ibid.*

30. *Ibid.*

31. *Ibid.*

32. Posted March 27, 2003.

33. Susannah Rosenblatt and James Rainey, "Katrina Rumors," *Los Angeles Times*, September 27, 2005; "True Crime," *Greater Baton Rouge Business Report*, September 15, 2005.

33. Susannah Rosenblatt and James Rainey, "Katrina Rumors," *Los Angeles Times*, September 27, 2005; "True Crime," *Greater Baton Rouge Business Report*, September 15, 2005.

34. *CBS Evening News*, August 7, 2002.

35. *Ibid.*

36. *Ibid.*

37. Allen Johnson, "To Catch a Killer," bestofneworleans.com, February 4, 2003.

38. Mustafa, *ibid.*

39. *CBS News*, *ibid.*

40. Cataldie, *ibid.*

41. *CNN*, "'Major Development' in Louisiana Serial Killer Case," January 23, 2003.

42. *Ibid.*

43. *Ibid.*

44. *Ibid.*

45. *Ibid.*

46. *Ibid.*

Chapter 4

The Birth of the Internet Social Movement in Baton Rouge

The information released by the Multi-Agency Task Force about the Baton Rouge serial murders in December, 2002 and January, 2003 was the most specific information yet released to the public, and it stimulated much discussion and theorizing by just about everyone who lived in Baton Rouge, south Louisiana and south Mississippi. The information was specific enough that it was possible for people to speculate about the type of person that the police were looking for, with most of the speculation having to do with the occupation of the killer. For others, the information released about the facial profile, the truck, and the kind of shoes being worn allowed them to think of specific individuals they knew who might end up being the serial killer. This information in turn prompted people to think retrospectively about encounters they had already experienced with strangers who might be the killer. People were not shy about sharing their hunches with the Task Force, judging from the overwhelming volume of calls to their tip line. But there was a need for more discussion, for more reaching out to others and for comparing notes and theories with other people.

The stage was thus set for Dr. Godwin's entry into the fray. Convinced that interest in the case had spiked enough to support a sustained discussion on the Internet, and having published his critique of the FBI's psychological profile of the suspect, Dr. Maurice Godwin started a *Yahoo!* discussion group in the early morning of January 15, 2003 with this description of the group: "This discussion group is focused on the Baton Rouge serial murders. The group exists solely for Baton Rouge community members to share and discuss aspects of the serial murders taking place in their city. To be considered for this list you must live in the Baton Rouge or Lafayette, Louisiana area or surrounding areas."[1] After that, he waited to see what the response would be.

How many people would sign up for the group? The founder didn't really know. He knew people were ready for such a group, but he had no idea what to expect. And he knew that there were competing groups, such as the one on *Court TV*.

Godwin didn't have to wait long to find out if anyone was interested. Immediately, the response was robust. About 100 people joined in the days after the group began, and it would eventually grow to more than 250 people, all local people or people with local interests as Dr. Godwin has specified. Probably without realizing it, he was suddenly in charge of a movement that would qualify as a postmodern social movement due to its emphasis on locality. It was later discovered that several people participating in Godwin's forum also signed up and participated in the alternative forums where locality was not a requirement for participation.

Dr. Godwin played many roles as moderator. He was a teacher, disciplinarian, negotiator, promoter, timekeeper, inspiration, and at times, a person that was refreshingly open minded about various theories regarding the case. As long as the theories fit the known facts of the case at that time and were reasonably in line with what Predator was telling him, he was willing to consider them as a possibility. And he hated it when speculation rambled far from the known facts, and this is where the disciplinarian role came in. As he wrote on March 19:

> I approve all messages that are posted to this list. A member tried to post the photo/message of that guy (Mary Kuntz Email) however, I rejected it. This list will not become another *Court TV* list.[2]

In this particular case, Mary Kuntz was posting a photo of a possible suspect on the *Court TV* discussion and Godwin would not allow the picture to be posted to his group as it was purely speculative and only remotely in line with any known facts in the case. On other occasions he cautioned:

> There's no information to support that Pam Kinamore was posed. Let's end this particular discussion.[3]

No more speculation about any victims and if they were held captive. There's no evidence to suggest this is the case.[4]

Some of the comments are getting far fetched. Stay with facts only or close to the facts.[5]

I will not let the tone of the messages get out of hand. I let several through to wake some members up but I have a fairly good handle on the situation.[6]

Compliance with his guidelines got recognized, too, as he wrote on April 14: "I would like to say 'thank you' to all the members of this list for making it the first and only 'honest' and most factual' discussion list available for the community members in Baton Rouge."[7]

Dr. Godwin also encountered situations in which he had to be protector of the group. When it was thought possible that the serial killer had actually joined Dr. Godwin's electronic group and was "trolling" for potential victims in the "member's section" of the site, he turned off the function that allowed group members to look at or to check out some of the personal data of the group's members. This decision was made sometime during the spring of 2003. Godwin's motives were good and he seemed genuinely to care for the women of Baton Rouge, on one occasion posting some safety tips for women.[8] No doubt his specific reason for turning off the members' section of the group was that he remembered an earlier case he had worked on, that of John Edward Robinson, Sr, the first known Internet serial killer. Robinson lured his victims though Internet chat rooms and killed them, continuing to cash their government checks or alimony payments for years with just minimal interference from desperate families and frustrated investigators.[9]

Godwin also let the group know about breaking leads and situations that might be threatening to Baton Rouge women. After he learned of an abnormally large purchase of UPS uniforms by persons unknown, he wrote: "There has been a huge purchase ($32,000) of United Parcel Service (UPS) uniforms on eBay over the last (30) thirty days. This represents a serious threat as bogus drivers can drop off anything to anyone with deadly consequences. When a UPS driver appears at your door, make absolutely sure they are driving a UPS truck. UPS does not make deliveries or pick-ups in anything except company vehicles and they should be able to furnish a VALID I.D."[10] The message continued: "Installation ID checks and security checks ensure personnel on station are authorized to be there. ID checks should be conducted for home deliveries. Personnel are reminded to keep their family members informed and remind them to be suspicious of home deliveries, suspicious personnel and vehicles in the area, and items that seem 'out of place.' If you have a problem, IMMEDIATELY call security or your State/local Law enforcement."[11]

Early speculation in the Baton Rouge case diverged in two directions at once. First there was open speculation about the occupation of anyone who could possibly gain entry to a woman's home without using bodily force, as appeared to have happened to several victims of the serial killer. UPS drivers were immediately suspect, but the discussion ran the gamut of construction workers; telephone, utility and cable repairmen; policemen; recreation workers; delivery men (Postal Service, FedEx, florists, pizza men, and others); and people who work door to door such as salesmen, political operatives, and religious workers. Second, and often in conjunction with the first line of speculation, people nominated certain individuals that they knew from personal experience who fit the psychological profile that was presented by the Task Force. Just about everyone in the discussion group probably knew someone who fit the profile or displayed enough anti social characteristics to be considered a legitimate candidate for serial killer. As these people were likely to be anti-social and mean, it did not take long for a series of possible suspects to be identified and then relayed to the discussion group.

Because the entries to the victims' homes were unforced, people began to generate lists of the kinds of people or occupational workers that might be able to talk themselves into a woman's home without arousing any suspicion. For example, there was early theorizing about men working for BREC, the Baton Rouge Recreation and Park Commission for the Parish of East Baton Rouge.

BREC operates 184 community parks in East Baton Rouge and employs administrative personnel and recreation specialists as well as a variety of manual workers such as equipment operators, irrigation technicians, landscape workers, maintenance workers, and a plethora of janitors and miscellaneous laborers to clean up after all the activities. Seasonal workers may also be hired as activity instructors, for example, as tennis instructors.[12] Given this massive presence, the appearance of a BREC maintenance truck in the community would normally not create much alarm, but in the fearful and emotionally tense aftermath of the serial killings, the appearance of the trucks became objects of suspicion.

There were BREC facilities close to the scene of the Green and Pace murders. One BREC facility was only one third of a mile from the Green residence and the other was located 1 mile from the Pace residence. According to the "BREC theory" as argued in Dr. Godwin's discussion group by several advocates, the appearance of the worker in the neighborhood would not arouse suspicion, and the worker could open his conversation with a stranger by saying that he was trying to find the owners of lost items in the park such as a purse, or cash, or a cell phone. Moreover, the worker would know "the lay of the land" in the neighborhoods close to the BREC facilities, including knowledge of the apartments or homes where a body could be transported out without being seen or without arousing much suspicion.[13] In essence, the BREC workers were in a position to do a crude and unschooled estimate of the type of "landscape analysis" that Dr. Godwin often performed after the fact of a particular murder. BREC had also been on the public mind ever since the Leroy McCutcheon case in Baton Rouge that was eventually solved in 1997. McCutcheon's murder victim had been found in a BREC park in 1985.[14]

Utility workers such as meter readers were also singled out for increased scrutiny as they performed their jobs. A member of the Multi-Agency Task Force living in Lafayette told residents there that the safest thing to do when you receive an unscheduled call is not open the door, and to confirm that person's employment. He noted that people with concerns should call Lafayette Utilities System, Cox Cable, UPS, FedEx, floral companies, restaurants and any other company that delivers before opening a door.[15] Florists in Lafayette were reporting no problems with delivery, but supervisors of meter readers indicated that they had been questioned by people as they were doing their jobs.[16]

Local police and state troopers were also in the spotlight as it is known that people naturally submit to law enforcement officers and generally acquiesce to their demands as authority figures, even in instances where people have things to hide. For example, in several of the "search and seizure" incidents that became famous Fourth Amendment constitutional law cases, the persons under suspicion willingly opened their cars or property up to inspection by officers, apparently not knowing that a citizen has a right to refuse such searches or to limit them. His or her acquiescence to the officer's request, if not coerced, amounts to a waiver of the citizen's Fourth Amendment protection against unreasonable searches and seizures.[17] This being the case, it was reasoned that a similar social dynamic could take place if the serial killer was a real cop, or someone who had gotten access to a police uniform and was using it and posing as an officer who presents himself at people's residences on official business. If he asks to come inside, and does nothing to arouse our suspicion, few would question his legitimacy. Discussion group members disagreed, however, about whether the killer was a cop in disguise. One writer relayed what Louisiana State Representative Yvonne Welch told a rally of victims of the serial killer:

> … Welch said she wanted police to submit to DNA testing to reassure the public they weren't the killer. "A lot of ladies are telling me that they don't feel comfortable with the police. They're afraid that a police officer may be the serial killer, in fact," Welch said. "They're telling me that if they're driving at night and a police officer puts on their lights to stop them, they're afraid."[18]

Regular contributor, DF, disagreed:

> I doubt the sk is a uniformed policeman, mailman, etc. Based on the high probability that he has murdered at least 13 more than the five connected with DNA, I would say the sk has been at it for 10-15 years or so. I don't think he could keep murdering in anonymity if he were wearing a uniform. If he has committed 10 or more murders, the uniform would have come to light by now, the odds would be that someone saw a uniform (which would have drawn attention).[19]

One real life officer got so much attention and came under such intense suspicion that he was asked to be swabbed, and his refusal to do so ended up as a court case.[20] At the height of this controversy, there were public calls for all law enforcement officers to be swabbed to rule out the officers as candidates for serial killer, just as Yvonne Welch had suggested.[21] Englade refused, not wanting to set a precedent for the blanket swabbing of a category of citizens.[22]

Rumors continued to swirl, however, that a cop was the serial killer. Several incidents appeared to fuel the fires of these rumor mills. The first occurred Monday, March 24, at about 5:00 P.M. A 30-year old black female reported that she was home alone when she heard a knock at her door. When she asked who it was, a man replied that he was a police officer. The woman looked outside through a window and saw a man with what appeared to be a police cap and jacket standing at her door. She opened her door slightly and the man told her he needed to come inside and ask her a few questions. He was carrying a notepad in one hand. The woman allowed the man in. Once inside, he put the notepad into his pocket and grabbed the victim by the throat. The suspect and the victim struggled, and at some point the suspect retrieved a piece of cloth from his pocket and placed it over her mouth and nose. The victim reported the cloth had a sharp chemical smell. Continuing to struggle, she finally got her hands on her hot curling iron, striking the suspect across the right cheek, possibly burning him and causing him to flee. The victim states she then observed the suspect get into a white car with dark windows and leave the area. The victim was treated at a local hospital for minor injuries.[23] After sitting on the information for a week, details of the woman's description of the attacker were released to the public.[24] Eventually, after DNA testing of the curling iron was completed, the suspect was ruled out as the serial killer, and the woman's report turned out not to be true.[25] The initial reports, however, only fueled the fears of the police that were already widespread in the community.

After a rally on the steps of the Louisiana capitol building in Baton Rouge, State Representative Jack Smith related how he had reminded the head of the Louisiana State Police at a legislative hearing that a serial rapist in Lafayette who struck between 1986 and 1997 was a 20-year police veteran. "I was a police officer for a number of years and unfortunately, as hard as we try through the interview process, every once in a while somebody slips through who shouldn't have gotten there," Smith said. "We might have a bad apple out there."[26] To make matters worse, a State Trooper was arrested in connection with an unsolved June, 2002 murder of an Alexandria woman.[27] The trooper was later cleared as a suspect in this case, but the initial arrest of the officer only confirmed peoples' worst fears that a few bad apples in law enforcement might be there not to serve and protect, but to prey upon the public.[28]

Medical personnel also became suspect as few would question their credentials, and several of the victims either worked for home health agencies or had some kind of connection to them. Gina Green was a Nurse specializing in infusion therapy who worked for HSC Infusion out of Lafayette, a home health care service. At the time of the serial killings, they had a Baton Rouge office on Industriplex which is almost parallel with Briarwood Place where Pam Kinamore lived. Kinamore's husband was in a wheelchair due to an accident which happened prior to their marriage, and may have needed home health care.[29] Employees must be strong enough to lift someone in a wheelchair. Randi Mebruer of Zachary, whose death was similar to that of the Baton Rouge cases, also worked for a home health agency out of Lafayette.[30] One group member commented that whether these apparent connections are coincidental or not, law enforcement should begin an investigation. How many other kinds of people would come into contact with the victims would make an interesting flowchart. Even random or incidental contacts could be important.[31]

As some of the killer's victims were dumped outside near bodies of water and oftentimes at night to avoid detection, one poster to the group suspected an "outdoorsman type," one whose work or recreation involves frequent time spent outdoors in rugged settings. This person wrote:

> I haven't seen the "dump" sites, but my impression is that most of them (and I'm including some of the murders not attributed to the SK) are typical South Louisiana terrain, which is to say wet, bug and snake-infested and very dense. I asked four guys at work today if any of them would step off the road and go 200 or 300 yards into the woods for any reason at night, and all said they couldn't imagine doing that. I would think very few people would consider that a comfortable situation.
>
> So that says to me the guy must be (or have been as a young person) a hunter, camper, fisherman or Cajun.[32]

Several in the discussion group observed that the killings tended to happen on or near holidays, or at low traffic times in or near the LSU campus. This suggested that the killer was smart enough to attack at times he was less likely to be noticed, and suggested to some that he may work a more or less conventional 40 hour work week from Monday through Friday. The following is information posted to the group regarding the LSU schedule and the times that victims were abducted or murdered:

Green: 9/23/01, This was a Sunday, no classes at LSU.

Pace: 5/31/02, This was a Friday, one week after graduation (5/24) between spring and summer semesters; although some classes for intersession were going on, for the most part, the campus would have been relatively empty of students.

Kinamore: 7/12/02: Friday, last day for session B of summer school; session A still going on; still far fewer students on campus during this time of the year than fall or spring semesters.

Colomb: 11/23/02: I think this date is correct?? This was the Saturday before LSU Thanksgiving break the following Thursday & Friday. Even though classes were held Mon, Tues & Wed of Thanksgiving week, many students go out of town that week, so this too would have been a time when fewer students were on campus, which may or may not be significant since Colomb was in Lafayette when abducted (unless the sk is an LSU student or employee).[33]

Another contributor similarly noted:

I was watching WAFB this morning and they had an interview with a Criminologist from LSU. She drew an interesting connection that I had never truly realized. She said that what stands out in her mind is that most, if not all, of the proven victims of the BRSK as well as some of those thought to be victims of the BRSK have been abducted around holidays. She went into detail, but to be honest, I don't remember them all. There were 2 during Memorial Day week; Yoder during Mardi Gras; Fowler at Christmas; Columb at Thanksgiving (I think that Kinamore was around July 4th).[34]

Other contributors disagreed, arguing that it was not so much a matter of holidays as a matter of increased opportunities to attack when the campus is quiet. As one person noted:

The SK's attacks aren't linked directly to holidays or days of the week; they are brought about by increased opportunity for him to attack successfully. Times when the campus is relatively quiet and there are fewer people around to witness an attack are times of increased opportunity for the SK.

You almost have to live in South Baton Rouge near LSU to know how much football affects the lives of people on and near campus. Gina Wilson Green was killed on an off weekend when there was no football game! Students go home en masse when there is no football game for entertainment, so the campus is deserted.

I went to the official LSU Sports Net web site to see the 2001 football schedule:

09/01/01 Tulane (TigerVision) Baton Rouge, La. 7 p.m.
09/08/01 Utah State Baton Rouge, La. 7 p.m.
09/29/01 Tennessee (ESPN) Knoxville, Tenn. 6:45 p.m.

Carrie Yoder was killed during Mardi Gras holiday; campus deserted; increased opportunity.

Dene Colomb's killing remains the unusual one; she was killed just before Thanksgiving.

Pam Kinamore was killed just after LSU's summer school session ended. (Summer school schedules are complicated, but I can post the 2002 schedule if anyone wants to see it).

Charlotte Murray Pace and Christine Moore were both killed between terms at LSU in May 2002.

BE CAREFUL! Watch your friends and your teenage daughters![35]

As many of the killings occurred near the LSU campus, there was much suspicion that the serial killer was a professor, graduate assistant, or fellow student who might have been known to the victims and who might have been able to enter the victims' residences without a struggle. This became known as the "LSU Theory." A student who finds one of their professors on their door step likely would allow that person to enter their home.

The data on killings in or around LSU was supportive of the idea that there had been multiple serial killers on campus for decades. Eleven women with ties to the University community or the Baton Rouge serial killer had been murdered during a 22 year period. Five were linked by DNA evidence and most had lived near the campus or had some recent contact with LSU. The families of Christine Moore and Geralyn DeSoto, murdered in 2002, believed they also were victims of the serial killer, but in 2002 there is no scientific evidence to link them. DeSoto, but not Moore, would later be connected to Derrick Lee by DNA, and Lee would eventually be convicted of DeSoto's death in his first trial.[36]

Four of the cases that were unsolved as of the spring of 2003 had striking similarities to the more recent victims tied to Derrick Lee. In November, 1981, LSU student Eleanor Parker, 19, disappeared while driving to her apartment on Gardere Lane. Police found her car on the side of the road one week later near the former downtown Goudcheaux's, Parker's place of employment. Officials said there was no evidence of a struggle. She has not been found, and no leads have developed since her disappearance. Then, in October, 1985, geology graduate student Melissa Montz, 27, disappeared during a jog on Brightside Lane. Her skeletal remains were found November 25 near the LSU golf course, south of the Nicholson-Burbank Extension. More recently in 1997, Eugenie Boisfontaine disappeared while walking around the LSU lakes. Her driver's license, credit cards and keys were found during the next three days. Her body was found in August of 1997 in Bayou Manchac with a skull fracture. Police said there was no indication of a break-in at Boisfontaine's house on Stanford Avenue.[37] Finally, Kassie Lynne Federer, 19, was found shot to death inside her Garden District apartment on September 13, 1999. Someone kicked in the front door and killed her with a small caliber gun. Her killer has not been found.[38]

Interest in the LSU theory was riding high when the following incident took place, one that may not have drawn a lot of attention except for a possible LSU connection to the serial killings. A member of the group posted the news story verbatim:

> An LSU instructor has been cited with simple battery after being accused of punching a student following a weekend chase on campus.
>
> The student, whose name was not released, told LSU police that a man on a motorcycle followed him into a parking lot behind the student union Saturday afternoon. He says the man walked up to his car, told him to lower his window and then punched him in the face.
>
> LSU Police Captain Ricky Adams says a witness in the student's car confirmed the story. Officers tied the motorcycle license plate to 52-year-old Mark Slovak. During questioning, Slovak admitted to swiping sunglasses off the driver's face. Adams issued a misdemeanor summons for simple battery. He says the D.A.'s office likely will contact Slovak later this week. He could face a fine, probation or jail if found guilty.
>
> Slovak says he teaches motorcycle safety classes and how to avoid the kinds of reckless driving he faced Saturday. He says the student made an illegal U-turn and missed hitting him by an inch. Then, he says the student laughed and made an obscene gesture. Adams says the student told police he may have cut off the motorcycle.
>
> Slovak is director of the LSU Physics Tutoring Center and runs the Department of Physics and Astronomy's planetarium. He has received two teaching awards and is contracted to teach through 2004. He could learn today whether he faces any disciplinary action by the university.[39]

This lead went nowhere, however, and the group was left to pursue other candidates.

The easy, unforced access to the victims also suggested that the killer may have had an innocent looking or innocent sounding pretense for entering someone's home. If so, the killer was very convincing. This brought to mind a number of religious groups with door to door ministries such as Church of Christ, the Mormons, and especially Jehovah's Witnesses, who have largely become famous due to their practice of a door to door ministry. One person wrote to the group: "Be aware of religious folks who knock on doors, or people who seem to be such. How easy it would be to masquerade as an LDS or Jehovah's Witness. Many people will open their doors for these."[40]

One of the more interesting aspects of the Internet social movement was the open and honest discussion of such possibilities. Some discussants openly suggested that the "Witness angle" or "Witness theory" was legitimate while others vigorously objected. When debates of this kind became too vigorous or too personal, Dr. Godwin would have to intervene.

The advocates of this particular theory might have been people that had grown tired of the constant irritating visits from the Witnesses, or who had long suspected that the real purpose of the visits was to hustle funds for the organization. There was suspicion too that the Witnesses were dividers, trying to conquer young people and then separate them from their families. They are generally despised in heavily French Catholic south Louisiana, where families have been Catholic for generations and folks are basically immune to efforts of other religions to convert them. With all this negativity, they were an easy target. And with reports of deviancy in and around the Catholic Church and other religions, it was not much of a stretch even for Catholics to believe that a "religious" person can lead a double life and might not be who they seem to be. One message posted to the discussion group stated that the person of interest drawing released in January, 2003 revealed a "weak" person, someone who might have been a "Bible quoter."[41]

The objections in this case came from one of the discussion group participants whose family was largely composed of Jehovah's Witnesses. He defended the unpopular Witnesses, saying that it was unlikely that a serial killer could pass as a normal or legitimate person in their religious group given the rigid conduct norms of the group and the close scrutiny that members face from the local congregation elders. Furthermore, the Witnesses do most of their preaching on the doorstep and it is somewhat unusual for them to enter homes, or even to ask to enter unless directly invited by a homeowner or "householder" in the lexicon of the Witnesses. The poster also instructed the group about how the Witnesses operate; how they meet initially at a local Kingdom Hall to form "car groups," and from there, go door to door in groups of two or more to minister to people. Thus, it would be somewhat unusual for Witnesses to work by themselves, as a killer embedded in their ranks would have to work. The poster also noted the usual dress and appearance of the Witnesses, and how any variations from that protocol would be distressing internally to Witnesses within their organization. Basically, the purpose of the post was to defend the Witnesses and other door to door groups and to express the unlikelihood of the attacker belonging to such a group of people. It was also an attempt to illustrate what normal Witness activity was like, and how someone posing as a Witness would stand out and appear different, at least according to the norms of the Witnesses.[42] This posting ended with some advice:

IF SOMEONE APPROACHES YOUR DOOR ALONE AND IS NOT WELL DRESSED AND WELL GROOMED, AND NOT CARRYING A LITERATURE BAG, AND CLAIMS TO BE A JEHOVAH'S WITNESS, THIS PERSON MAY NOT BE A WITNESS, THIS PERSON MAY BE AN IMPOSTER!! PLEASE, PLEASE, BE CAREFUL!!

A true Jehovah's Witness will not be offended if you do not answer a knock on your door. Witnesses today have alternative forms of witnessing such as telephone witnessing, and they fully understand people's fears about safety and security.

Witnesses are kind and gentle people who enjoying speaking with others about the Bible. Let's not drag them into this sordid mess about the Baton Rouge SK.

It is unlikely, however, that Witnesses will curtail their door to door ministry. Often it is accelerated in times of trouble when people are grieving.[43]

A sympathetic member of the group responded:

What I thought of when the question of non-threatening people came up is this: If a young man came to my door wearing a white shirt and black slacks with a bicycle helmet saying he was a Church of Latter Day Saints (Mormon) missionary and that his partner had been struck by a car down the street and no one else had answered their door, I wouldn't have been overly suspicious in times past. Especially in the daytime, I might open my door just to peer down the street. That's all the SK needs.

No one is (or should be, anyway) pointing fingers at specific denominations. In fact, the point is that these are all people we trust because all the ones we've met before have been good, good people.

It pains me to see yet more badness grow from the SK's evil.[44]

After generating a modest discussion, someone wrote that it is probably the best and the safest strategy of all not to open the door for anyone. This was a point on which everyone could agree.[45] After that, the group moved on to other theories. Oddly enough, Derrick Lee was conducting Bible studies in Atlanta at the time that he was arrested.[46]

The other direction taken was to identify individuals who fit the anti social personality profile being constructed by the Task Force. Here, the posters were often identifying ex-spouses, workmates, and others that they had met that they just didn't like and that they thought fit the profile very well. Some of the candidates were carefully thought out, as one poster noted when he nominated a local sports referee as a possible serial killer candidate.

As presented by the poster, this person was a winter sports referee suspected to be living off a settlement check or retirement check plus the residual income from referring games or matches in the Baton Rouge and Lafayette. This man's life appeared to be much as the FBI profile had suggested: a person on fixed income and of limited means. Further, the pattern of the killings just happened to be for the most part before or after the winter sports season, and this particular individual's personality, as the poster had learned from a few unpleasant interactions, was definitely anti social enough to warrant consideration by the Task Force. The poster presented the "referee theory" to the group and gleefully called in the individual's name to the Task Force.

The trick here was to present to the group a profile of the person who was a candidate without giving away enough personal information that so that the angry candidate can sue the poster later. In the above case, after interviewing the person who posted this message, I learned that the poster knew privately more than was being revealed to the group. He knew exactly which sport the man refereed (it was high-school wrestling) and the poster knew from very painful personal experience that the candidate did have several of the psychological characteristics revealed by the Task Force. Moreover, the individual (the candidate) had managed to attach himself to a national wrestling organization and thus his opinion about the sport carried much weight in Louisiana although almost universally he is disliked statewide by the wrestling community, at least in the view of this particular poster. A history of the sport in Louisiana, written by a coach in Baton Rouge, does not even mention the man's name. Despite this, he boldly and quite abrasively claims to be an expert on wrestling in Louisiana. The poster also knew that this individual lived about one mile from Dene Columb and refereed many matches in Baton Rouge including some at Lee High School, very close to the geographic area being predicted by Predator as an area where the serial killer would soon strike once again. Due to an abundance of caution, this amount of detail about the candidate was not shared with the discussion group. The poster wanted to avoid a "Mary Kuntz" kind of situation where information was being shared irresponsibly. Kuntz published a photo and detailed information about her candidate on the *Court TV* forum with little to go on except that he resembled the person of interest photo.[47] Dr. Godwin made it clear that he did not support such irresponsible speculation.

Elsewhere, it was obvious that other people were doing much the same as the poster of the referee theory: seeing someone in the community that might fit the profile and calling that person in to the Task Force, and/or posting their theory to Dr. Godwin's discussion group. Dr. Godwin would then opine about the theory given what was known by him about the victims and the geographic patterns of the killings. He was remarkably open minded about some, including the referee theory which he thought had potential. Obviously, too, a number of people were simply nominating people out of their hatred for them: bosses, ex spouses and ex lovers. This was less well thought out and more an emotional reaction than a well thought out theory. For example, a few female members of the group nominated ex spouses or ex boyfriends that had been or were currently stalking them, and were considered dangerous. One contributor shared this scenario:

I have someone in mind, (I have called the tip line). The weird thing is that he is married BUT his wife is pretty whacked too and is a complete enabler. She could very well be afraid of him. They never had a normal marriage dynamic. She was really more like a mother that left him when he was ten. Anyway, I can't imagine a woman (or man) in the world who would hesitate to open the door to her. She is a pleasant, sweet-looking woman with a lovely smile.

I don't know if they still live in BR but they have lived for many years in the LSU area and are very familiar with the Lafayette area as well.

I wouldn't think that a wife would be in on something like this. Is it possible? All of it is hard to imagine. This makes sense, though. She would be the perfect bait for a trap. And this guy is psycho enough (and smart enough) to do this sort of thing.[48]

Amidst all the speculation, the citizens of Baton Rouge received the worst possible news that they could imagine. After waiting a reasonable amount of time, Carrie Yoder's boyfriend Lee Stanton reported Yoder missing on March 5.[49] The community's worst fears were coming true as everyone waited word on what had happened to the promising LSU student.

ENDNOTES

1. From the front page of the discussion group.

2. Posted March 19, 2003.

3. Posted March 25, 2003.

4. Posted March 23, 2003.

5. Posted March 25, 2003.

6. Posted April 2, 2003.

7. Posted April 14, 2003.

8. Posted March 18, 2003.

9. Sue Wiltz and Maurice Godwin, *Slave Master*. New York: Pinnacle, 2004.

10. Posted April 7, 2003.

11. *Ibid.*

12. This information is from the BREC web site at www.brec.org.

13. Messages posted to the discussion group on March 29, April 8 and April 9, 2003.

14. Karl Kretzer, *Danced to Death: The Desperate Hunt for a Cross-Country Serial Killer*. Baltimore: PublishAmerica, 2005.

15. Posted March 20, 2003.

16. *Ibid.*

17. See, for example, *Schneckloth v. Bustamonte*, 418 U.S. 218 (1973).

18. Posted March 27, 2003.

19. Posted March 26, 2003.

20. See, for example, Susan Finch, "Baton Rouge Man Sues for his DNA." *New Orleans Times Picayune*, June 3, 2003.

21. *CBS News*, "A Serial Killer in Police Garb?" April 8, 2003.

22. Posted March 27, 2003.

23. Posted April 3, 2003.

24. *Ibid.*

25. Posted July 9, 2003.

26. Posted April 8, 2003.

27. Posted April 9, 2003.

28. Posted April 13, 2003.

29. Posted April 1, 2003.

30. Posted April 2, 2003.

31. Posted April 1, 2003.

32. Posted March 12, 2003.

33. Posted March 12, 2003.

34. Posted March 12, 2003.

35. Posted May 11, 2003.

36. Posted March 22, 2003.

37. *Ibid.*

38. *Ibid.*

39. Posted May 5, 2003.

40. Posted March 27, 2003.

41. Posted May 4, 2003.

42. Posted March 30, 2003.

43. *Ibid.*

44. Posted March 30, 2003.

45. Posted March 26, 2003.

46. Stanley, *ibid.*

47. Posted March 10, 2003.

48. Posted March 25, 2003.

49. Josh Noel and Emily Kern, "Carrie Yoder's Body Found in Whiskey Bay," *WBRZ*, March 14, 2003.

Chapter 5

The Death of Carrie Lynn Yoder

The sense of moral outrage among citizens in Baton Rouge, south Louisiana, and south Mississippi appeared to escalate exponentially with word that Carrie Yoder was missing. Though no immediate link could be made between her disappearance and the serial killer, people were expecting the worst. The outrage over even the possibility of a potential link began to ramp up instantly after the announcement that she had been absent from her home for over two days. I believe that the raw messages posted to Dr. Godwin's discussion group are a far better indicator or portrayal of this outrage than any words that I could find to describe it. For example, a Mississippian known to the discussion group as "Miss Ellie" wrote:

> This is just unbelievable!! IF this body turns out to be Yoder's ... this is just unbelievable!! If the people in Baton Rouge are not outraged I just don't know what else could possibly make them be!! Something drastic needs to be done. Being in Mississippi, my mom and sisters called me just a little while ago to tell me the news. I will be waiting to get the latest via internet. Unbelievable!!![1]

A few days later, local news confirmed the awful truth that the body recovered in Whiskey Bay was that of Carrie Yoder, a graduate student at Louisiana State University.[2] DNA evidence would link Yoder's killer to the murders of Gina Green, Pam Kinamore, Charlotte Pace, and Dene Colomb. East Baton Rouge Parish Coroner Louis Cataldie said Yoder died of asphyxiation caused by strangulation and was beaten by the killer.[3]

As word spread that the body was indeed Yoder's, several messages posted in the discussion group left little room for doubt about how local women felt. The message below posted in all capital letters is just one example. In discussion groups, messages in "all caps" are typically viewed as a form of "shouting" one's message.

WOMEN ALL OVER SOUTHEASTERN LOUISIANA ARE LIVING IN TERROR. OUR DAUGHTERS, SISTERS, MOTHERS, AND FRIENDS ARE BEING SYSTEMATICALLY AND HORRIFICALLY MURDERED BY THE BATON ROUGE SERIAL KILLER.

PLEASE HELP TO STOP THE MADNESS...MANY HAVE EX-PRESSED A REAL CONCERN THAT ALTHOUGH THEY BELIEVE THE BATON ROUGE POLICE DEPARTMENT ARE DOING ALL THEY CAN, THEY DO NOT HAVE THE RESOURCES OR THE EX-PERTISE THAT IS VITAL TO CATCH THIS KILLER. WE NEED HELP FROM OUR PUBLIC OFFICIALS AND BUSINESS AND COMMUNITY LEADERS TO OBTAIN ADDITIONAL FEDERAL INTERVENTION AND RESOURCES, WE NEED EXPERTISE FROM SERIAL KILLER EXPERTS OUTSIDE OF LOUISIANA AND MOST IMPORTANTLY, THE COOPERATION OF THE BATON ROUGE POLICE DEPARTMENT TO WORK WITH THE INDIVIDUALS WHO HAVE THE EXPERTISE TO HELP END THIS NIGHTMARE.

PLEASE WRITE TO THE GOVERNOR, YOUR SENATORS, YOUR STATE REPRESENTATIVES, YOUR CONGRESSMEN, YOUR BUSINESS AND COMMUNITY LEADERS; ASK YOUR FRIENDS TO DO THE SAME. THE BELOW COURTESY EMAIL ADDRESSES ARE THOSE OF INDIVIDUALS (MEMBERS OF THE LOUISIANA HOUSE AND SENATE) AND OTHER PUBLIC OFFICIALS) WHO COULD MAKE A DIFFERENCE AND I ASK THAT WHEN YOU FORWARD THIS EMAIL TO EVERYONE YOU KNOW THAT YOU CARBON COPY THIS TO EACH AND EVERYONE ON THE BELOW DISTRIBUTION LIST SO THAT YOUR VOICE CAN BE HEARD. DO IT FOR GINA GREEN, CHARLOTTE MURRAY PACE, PAM KINAMORE, DENE COLOMB AND CAR-RIE YODER AS HE HAS SILENCED THEIR VOICES .....

PLEASE DON'T LET THEIR DEATHS BE IN VAIN. DO IT FOR YOURSELF, YOUR DAUGHTERS, YOUR MOTHER, YOUR SIS-TERS, YOUR FRIENDS, BECAUSE WE ARE THE WOMEN HE IS STALKING NOW, ANY ONE OF US COULD BE HIS NEXT VIC-TIM. WE DON'T HAVE TO BE VICTIMS. THE WOMEN OF LOU-ISIANA DESPERATELY NEED AND DESERVE TO HAVE OUR PUBLIC OFFICIALS DO THE RIGHT THING AND INTERVENE IN THIS CRISIS.

PLEASE, PLEASE, GET INVOLVED, GET EVERYONE YOU KNOW INVOLVED, SO THAT THE KILLING WILL STOP.[4]

The courtesy email addresses of several Louisiana state representatives were printed at the end of this memo.

Not much time elapsed before Dr. Godwin weighed in with his own feelings about the case, in particular the failure of the Task Force to take his advice. His tone was much more measured as might be expected from an academic expert, though at times some anger appeared to flare up:

I have repeatedly stated openly through the media in Baton Rouge and my web site, that serial killers often revisit their previous victims' body disposal locations and that they should look in water for any future victims. As such, I do not think that the police or task force ever put one boat in the water near where victim 3 was found in order to look for Ms. Yoder. Also, they should have staked out the area around the Whiskey Bay bridge, if in fact the FBI profilers had correctly informed them of how serial killers often return back to previous dump locations. Of course, that is another story. If I had been on the task force as a consult-ant, they would have been told to put a surveillance on the bridge near Whiskey Bay, because serial killers often return to previous disposal sites to leave more victims and/or to psychologically reflect about the crimes.[5]

Dr. Godwin did not allow his frustration to slow his work; in fact, he appeared to be more motivated than ever to find the killer. Following fresh leads from his home in Fayetteville, North Carolina, Godwin asked his group on April 7: "Anyone aware of the break-in at the College Town apartments on Sunday, which is at the corner of Burbank and E. Boyd? This is not far from Carrie Yoder's house."[6]

Parish Coroner Louis Cataldie had to put a lot of the questions as well as the emotions he had about the serial killer case in the back of his mind while he was called to do his job as Coroner. Performing his autopsy the same day Yoder was found to maximize evidence, Cataldie discerned that Yoder had been strangled, but not before being savagely beaten. While she was still alive, nine of her ribs were broken at the point where they connect with the spine. The broken bones punctured a lung and her liver. He knew that she had been alive at the time of the beating because of the hemorrhaging at the trauma sites. As he wrote in his memoir, "You don't actively bleed when you're dead."[7]

For others, the intense anger at the news of Yoder's fate was turned fairly quickly into constructive efforts to help the police by collecting information pertinent to the case which might be utilized immediately in the investigation. A person known to the group as Jomma, a poster of messages to Dr. Godwin's group and to the *Court TV* message board, shared with Dr. Godwin's group how he (or she) had aggressively and proactively shared with the Task Force information that she had that might lead to the identification of the serial killer:

> I gave IKE, head of the task force, on WEDNESDAY (March 5), face to face, info and places they might want to search. I drove to BR at their request, as I had given the Laf Task force this info on MONDAY (March 3). The BR police could not "find" my suspect Monday evening and assumed he was at Mardi Gras. When Carrie came up missing I had to drive up to BR immediately with a Det. from Opelousas and my info in hand. However ONCE I got there, they refused to even look at it.
>
> ISN'T THAT STRANGE? And they turned down my request to make copies. They claimed he was in the process of being eliminated, but I swore the whole way home.
>
> Carrie was still a missing person, if this guy was important enough to swab immediately and I have a remote location (wooded area, near Whiskey Bay) that this person owns, don't you think they could have QUESTIONED him and asked if it was ok to search his property, anything?? The info I gave them on Monday included a residential address that is walking distance from Carrie's and they both worked in the AG center/Grad school.
>
> I almost fainted when I heard about Carrie on Wednesday. I can put this guy everywhere.
>
> We believe him to be swabbed, but suddenly his swab test was canceled. Now BR refuses to return any phone calls to LAF. PD and Opelousas PD.
>
> I am besides myself.
>
> THIS IS A TRAVESTY.[8]

This message drips with the heartfelt and frantic concern of Jomma about the case. She (or he) had taken the time to travel to Lafayette and to Baton Rouge with information she thought was important. The message also indicates a trend that we will increasingly see as public interest escalates: a tendency of members of the discussion group to disclose ever more specific information about specific individuals, and in the process, the posters were risking the possibility that they may be sued later by an innocent person if their suspected individual candidate is not indeed the serial killer. One can see from the emotional tone of the above memo that the task of finding the killer had taken on a higher personal priority for the message posters than the risk that they may be sued later by an innocent person that they suspected of being the serial killer.

The phrase in Jomma's message, "They claimed that he was in the process of being eliminated ..." opens up a whole new chapter of controversy in the case. Due to public pressure, police had ventured out into the community to swab certain individuals whose names had been called in to the Task Force tip line. As results of the DNA tests came in, certain individuals whose DNA did not match that of any of the victims could be crossed off the list of suspects, or they could be "eliminated" as suspects in the case as Jomma wrote. While all that was well and good, the state now faced a shortage of qualified personnel to analyze the swabs for DNA matches with the serial killer's victims. There was apparently a large backlog of swabs to test, and there was also concern that the victim may have left his DNA in a "rape kit" that is used to examine rape victims. There was also a large backlog of such rape kits from previous crimes that could be examined.[9] All of this opened a torrent of criticism that the state was not doing enough to assist local police in solving the case.

Jomma's memo also showed that the "LSU Theory" was being kept alive, as Jomma's suspect appeared to be an LSU employee (the AG or Agricultural Center and the graduate school are parts of the university). Other posters to Dr. Godwin's group were also actively pursuing the LSU theory; one person suggested that all LSU facility workers should be questioned, that is, maintenance personnel, janitors, and related workers:[10]

I would assume, as part of a systematic approach, the TF would thoroughly check LSU facility service employees for possible suspects (just as they would look closely at graduate students who may have been working in the same area as Carrie Yoder). Maybe the sk could stalk Carrie, watching from an LSU warehouse across the street from her house, because he is an LSU facility service employee. They have access to the entire campus (master keys to all offices/room and the means to break in automobiles). However, I haven't heard of any such leads being followed. In the building where I work on campus (as well as Indian Mound Parking Lot, there has been quite a bit of theft, auto-break-ins, and reports of stalking. As a victim of these crimes, in my search for the perp, I have been made increasingly aware of the great number of facility workers who drive assorted white vehicles and have virtually free access to every office, classroom, etc. (including personal computers of faculty, grad students, employees, etc.) on campus. Any thoughts/info/feedback?

(Would love to get some fresh insight on my perp).

DF[11]

These particular individuals, it appears, had been not been emphasized very much in previous postings as it appeared that most of that prior interest had focused on faculty and graduate students at LSU.

In a message that was similar in some respects to Jomma's, DF complained about the handling of the DNA swab evidence and dared to reveal more specific information about a specific suspect despite potentially harsh legal consequences.

> As I continue to follow leads on my suspect, my "respect" for the task force grows thin. Each time I turn in another piece of info, I am told they will get to it as soon as possible. If it turns out that my suspect is the sk, then Carrie Yoder should not have died; he was swabbed for DNA 5 weeks ago, but the DNA sits on a shelf in a crime lab because of a huge backlog. Within the last couple of days I learned two pieces of information that I would call extremely significant circumstantial evidence in light of info already submitted on this guy:

> First, my suspect frequents a hunting camp located in Grosse Tete and even lives there periodically. Second, my suspect has a close relative who lives in Scott. It makes sense to me that the only way to narrow the apparently huge number of suspects is to work from the Lafayette angle and connect the dots to identified Baton Rouge suspects. We know the sk lives in BR. But he absolutely must have intimate knowledge of Grand Coteau and Scott. Thanks to so many of you who provided enough details about these areas, it hit me like a ton of bricks, that if we can find a good reason for any of the viable suspects we have (I imagine our group has a few), to have knowledge of Grand Coteau and Scott, then we can narrow the number of suspects/leads significantly. I have a few ideas for doing this:

> 1) One, get a roster of all students, past and present, who attended the Academy of the Sacred Heart (next to cemetery where Colomb was abducted right?) and look for names connected to suspects—female relatives or identified friends who may have attended the school (which sounds very upscale and elite, would have to be very wealthy).

> 2) Look in the Lafayette directory for family names of suspect (in my case this was easy, since the name is unusual; there was only one listed which happens to be a close relative of my suspect).

3) Look in directory for business associates or close friends of suspect. Bottom line: I think the key to solving this thing is to look at the anomaly of the sk's departure from typical patterns and find a connection between the anomaly, which in this case is the unique qualities of Colomb's abduction and murder (location, remoteness, the fact that familiarity with these areas would be limited to relatively few people) and identified suspects who likely live in Baton Rouge. Fortunately, Grand Coteau and Scott are smaller areas than Baton Rouge and have far fewer people, which makes data/information more manageable. It would be easier to search for a person, or type of employment, or any criteria that might fit the sk in this area and connect him to already identified suspects that live in Baton Rouge. Focusing on suspects which have a connection would definitely limit the number of viable suspects.

Other ideas? Please share. There are lots of good minds in this group. If we work together, we can find the sk. We've been asked to give info to the task force, but I think the info is given in bits and pieces and not put together for big pictures to form—the result: 1000 tips per day since Yoder's abduction. With well over 16,000 tips, one would think Baton Rouge was a breeding ground for psychopaths. So we have information overload and indiscriminant filing/storage (yes, it's information storage and DNA storage—to be used/accessed at a later date?? after how many murders??) Even if investigative techniques are the best, without appropriate information screening and triaging, we're doomed.

So it's up to us. I'm not suggesting that we all submit names of suspects, etc., but that we submit ideas for investigating and solving this thing! We have quite a wealth of info posted on this website, and some good minds to analyze it.[12]

This thoughtful memo not only gave some specific information about an individual, but it also suggested a rational way to approach the case so as to reduce the number of people under consideration: to view the Lafayette murder as an anomaly and to search for people having connections to Baton Rouge *and* to the area where Dene Colomb's body was found. The memo was also a "call to arms" of sorts to get members of the group motivated enough to do some analyses of their own and to think through the evidence that was being accumulated. She clearly indicated that the Task Force was not doing this. She (or he) appeared to indicate that members of the forum may have to do their own police work and essentially conduct their own investigations.

Some members of the discussion group that tried out DF's method were more certain than ever that their own pet theory was correct. For example, the individual that posted the "referee theory" (see chapter 3) discovered that the winter sports referee he suspected as the serial killer had once worked at a school in northwest Lafayette that was quite close to the Scott, Louisiana area where Dene Colomb's body had been found. According to DF's criteria, this individual should take a higher priority than other candidates in the Task Force investigation. The poster of the original message chose not to send a follow up memo to the discussion group or to the Task Force, fearing legal reprisal from the referee should he prove to be innocent.

The anger over Yoder's death also triggered collective action in the form of a constructive and organized activism. For example, on Sunday, March 16, 2003 the first "victims of unsolved murders" rally was held since the death of Carrie Yoder. The best attended rally since rallies began in 2002 demanded action from the police, government, business, churches, media, and women themselves. The implicit message was this: "if you don't help get this serial killer, we can make your life difficult."[13] The rally also served as a forum to comment on the Yoder case and how law enforcement was handling it.[14] Messages posted to Dr. Godwin's discussion group kept members fully informed of such current developments. The following is information compiled from media reports that was cross-posted to Dr. Godwin's discussion group.

Before a crowd estimated at 150-200 people, Lynne Marino, emotionally distraught over her daughter's murder, tearfully spoke about her absence. "Do you know what it is like to watch a 13-year-old finish grammar school without the love and support of his mom, that is always there," said Marino.[15]

The family of Charlotte Murray Pace, the serial killer's second confirmed victim was also present at the rally. Murray's sister, Sam Pace says her grief has now changed to anger. She said: "My family will never be the same. We have been ripped apart by this. And I am furious that this has continued to happen, that this continues to happen to other families. In that, I have moved from grief, to sadness, to anger."[16]

Her anger was shared by Mary Ann Fowler's son John Pritchett. Fowler had been missing since Christmas Eve, 2002, when she was abducted outside a Port Allen sandwich shop. Pritchett said, "I am pissed off! I'm tired of hearing we don't have anything new to tell you John. I'm mad! I'm mad because a 65-year-old woman can't stop on the side of the highway and buy a sandwich in a wide open parking lot in broad daylight."[17]

Although Baton Rouge Police Chief Pat Englade claimed that the Serial Killer Task Force was using all the resources available to them, some people at the rally disagreed. Pam Kinamore's brother in law, Ed White, asked: "What would it hurt to bring in these (outside) experts and let them listen to the evidence, share their ideas and share their insights? What would that hurt? This is insane to be rejecting that kind of support when the other day it was admitted by the Task Force spokesperson that they are learning as they go. We don't have the privilege to learn as we go. We need to learn from the people who have been there before."[18]

Shortly before the rally a preacher who had pledged to pray until the killer is caught held his second prayer service on River Road. Reverend Riley Harbor led his congregation at Ebenezer Baptist Church in prayer for the families of the serial killer's victims. The body of LSU graduate student Christine Moore was found behind his churchyard. Although police had not yet connected that killing to the serial killer's DNA, Reverend Harbor said that he believes that God can do what seems impossible for man. He remarked: "I know if he did it for Moses, I know if he did it for Daniel, he'll do it for me. We're not interfering with the authorities, we're just trying to help the authorities, and God just laid on my heart, if we really pray together, I bet before this year is out the serial killer will be caught."[19]

On the LSU campus the next day, Monday, March 17, a group of female students calling itself "Targets" was targeting the serial killer. Wearing bull's-eye targets around their necks, the group passed out a sketch of the person of interest in the Dene Colomb case, collected signatures for an awareness rally and discussed calling for a walkout "to call attention to how many women are concerned about what's going on," said an organizer who, like many women in town, did not want to be identified.[20] The students set up a table at Free Speech Alley outside the student union to share information about the case with others. The women told their fellow classmates about where they can go to print out the sketch so they too can plaster it in their homes, on their cars and in their offices. "A lot of people have not seen the sketch," said one student organizer. "The more people who actually see the sketch, the more likely it is he'll be caught. Hopefully, you get the word out, people start talking." Another student working at the table said more people need to be aware of the danger. "We've been walking around acting like it's not happening," she said. "How do you know you're not the next one?"[21]

Meanwhile, the next day, March 18, a petition drive by a new group, CASK or Citizens Against the Serial Killer, was further helping Baton Rouge women convert their anger into action and uniting women in the quest to nab the serial killer. The frustrated women were showing renewed vigor in doing something, anything, to help stop the slayings. "We don't want to sit and do nothing," said CASK's founder who organized a group of friends she met online at Godwin's site and the *Court TV* site. "The citizens are going to catch him. The police can't do it alone." One woman, who goes by the screen name Lady Medic, said that someone in the group said, "Let's get fliers and do a rolling billboard."[22]

The concept was eagerly embraced and CASK members started to plaster their cars with a sketch of a man police wanted to question. The group also passed out 1,000 copies of the sketch at the March 16 victims rally where families and friends of murdered loved ones and their supporters gathered at the Capitol to mourn their loss and keep the case before the public eye. Lady Medic remarked, "We hope they will give them to friends, take them to the office, put them up in grocery stores." She also noted that she has received more than 130 messages from people who wanted to get involved in her group, said she is confident police will eventually track down the killer with the help of the community. "He's going to get caught," she said. "He can only do it so long before he gets caught."[23]

The anger that was the motivating factor in this new activism stood out at this particular rally. Lady Medic said: "We started out scared. Then we were frustrated. Now we're just angry." Another member of the group, who wished to be identified only by her screen name, Stormy, said, "The fear has turned to rage now."[24]

Over at the State Capitol, Yvonne Dorsey-Welch said she planned to add an amendment to the state budget bill that would steer additional money toward the investigation. "I don't think any of my colleagues will object to something that will save lives of Louisiana women," Dorsey-Welch said. "I'm consumed with it. I want him caught."[25]

Elsewhere in Baton Rouge, fears of the serial killer during the month of March had led to an increase in gun sales in the city. With the news of Carrie Lynn Yoder's murder confirmed through DNA to be linked to the serial killer, gun sales in Baton Rouge were suddenly skyrocketing once again. Local gun dealers told the media that many, especially women, were taking safety matters into their own hands. Don Hogan, owner of Baton Rouge Police Supply, said the influx in business completely sold them out of all of their revolvers. Hogan said the majority of his customers lately have been ladies, most of which are college students. He says most of them prefer the revolver because its small size and the fact that it is easy to conceal.[26] According to East Baton Rouge Parish Coroner Louis Cataldie, the State Police was receiving over 400 requests per week for concealed handgun permits at the height of the serial killer scare.[27]

Aside from an increase in gun sales, mace was also flying out of the stores by the cases. However, one college student did not think mace is enough. "Mace is minimal protection. Now I'm looking at some firearms."[28] Authorities said this all too increasing practice could lead to problems down the line for students who feel the need to carry guns in their purses or in vehicles. Getting caught with a concealed firearm on LSU's campus carried a 5-year prison term. Campus police said they were getting calls from students and parents about safety and were offering alternatives to firearms. "Routinely we receive calls about--How do I protect myself? We obviously encourage people about the alternative programs such as rape aggression and defense offered by LSU and the city of Baton Rouge. Even up to the point of pepper spray for line of defense. We encourage people to go reasonable with safety aspects," said Captain Ricky Adams with the LSU Police Department. In light of all the guns being purchased by students one was bound to show up. However, as of March, 2003 no students had been arrested for carrying a gun.[29]

The fear level in Baton Rouge was also expressed by those signing up for self defense classes. As one writer commented on Godwin's forum:

I'm going tonight to the one (defense class) on Florida Blvd. I'm taking my two daughters with me. While it may not help in a true hands on struggle, it's sure to have some good common sense tips and simple ideas that women may not even think about. I was informed by the La. State Police Dept. that I cannot obtain a conceal carry permit until I've been a resident here for 6 months. Kinda puts me at a disadvantage huh? I just moved from N.C and the two states do not reciprocate the permits. I think exceptions are needed here!!!!! Any thoughts?[30]

Dr. Godwin tried to alleviate fears by posting his own set of safety rules:

Never make an exception to the common sense rule.

1. Never arrive home by yourself, with no one in your house and walk to the house.

2. If there is ever a chance you have to make an exception to the common sense rule, call several people on your cell phone and let them know where you're at and the particular situation (nothing has to be suspicious or anything to take this precaution). Stay on the cell phone until you're comfortable that all is clear and safe both on the walk from your vehicle and inside your house. These precautions should also be taken while you're out shopping or doing whatever.

3. Never believe that someone at the door is who he or she says they are they are: never. This includes a female too! Eleven percent of the serial killers that I researched were team killers where a female was involved.

4. Stay in lighted area when you're outside. My study on 107 American serial killers found that often college students who were victims of serial killers walked across part of the campus at night by themselves.

I have more of the 'never make an exception to the common sense rule' but I just wanted to share a few here. These along with others will be featured in a forthcoming book about my work and me.

Dr. G[31]

A group member affiliated with a self-defense firm offered his own advice:

Self Defense Pointers Provided By A.S.P. & W.A.S.P.

Vital Areas of the Body

Contrary to popular belief, the groin area is not the most effective area to attack when confronted with danger. Out of necessity, a man is going to "protect his parts" nowadays and a good solid shot is not always presented.

It is recommended, by the more practical defense courses, to attack the eyes or ears before resorting to a groin shot. Let's look at these individually:

*The Eyes: first and foremost, if your attacker can't see you, he cannot pursue you. You can attack the eyes using your natural weapons, those tenacious finger nails (Gouge the eyes! Don't be apathetic, this guy is out to hurt you... Hurt him first!), a chemical agent such as MACE/Pepper Spray, any aerosol, even the "Binaca Blast" (Yes, it stings like Hell!), coins (thrown at the face), keys (gouging), sand, gravel or dirt (thrown at face). Once you attack the eyes, resort to using the oldest form of self defense in history: Nikejutsu.....in other words run like your life depends on it.... IT DOES!

*The Ears: the best and most effective way to attack the ears is by cupping your hands as if to hold water in each. Take your hands and slap both ears as hard as you can. This will rupture the ear drums and cause temporary dysfunction. Lastly, use your Nikejutsu....

*The Groin: as I stated, this is sort of the last resort. Use this only if you know you can get a good shot in. I recommend using the edge of your hand to strike or just grab his cluster as hard as you can and try to take them with you before using ... what? our Nikejutsu....Now if you can't get a good shot on his parts, or he simply has no nuts (literally) just above them is the bladder. Striking this area will cause similar pain as well as make him wet his pants...

I hope this tidbit of info is helpful to you ladies (and gents even) in your personal mission to stay safe.

If you like, I can make this an ongoing thread....

Support Our Boys and Girls![32]

Encouraged by the rise in awareness of the serial killer and increasingly tolerant publicity for its cause, CASK produced its first newsletter which was forwarded for all in the group to view and comment upon. Some members of CASK were also members of Dr. Godwin's group.

Citizens Against the Serial Killer

Fighting the War Against Women. No more murders!

PO Box 78398, Baton Rouge, Louisiana 70837

cask_br@...

Wow! The response to CASK has been overwhelming. We have received hundreds of e-mails from across the country, from people wanting to know how they can help. It has been incredible!

This is a loaded newsletter. Included you will find the CASK response to the Baton Rouge Task Force Press Conference held March 21, 2003. It has been sent to numerous news organizations through out the country. Also, are announcements with everything CASK has going on right now, including an upcoming rally this coming Thursday along with meetings in the works. There is a lot of stuff here.

If there are any suggestions or ideas, please send them to us.

Press Release

C.A.S.K. Response to Baton Rouge Task Force News Conference

Friday, March 21, 2003

Citizens Against the Serial Killer (C.A.S.K.) understands completely the incredible workload the Task Force must bear, especially since it has the added burden of dealing with the "non-traditional" serial killer that has crossed all barriers related to age, race and method of murder. We also have no doubt the Task Force is doing a fine job collecting the evidence necessary to obtain a conviction should this individual be captured.

However, as tax paying members of this community and potential victims of the serial killer, C.A.S.K. is deeply saddened and dismayed by the announcement that the investigation by the Task Force appears to have moved in a backward direction. The Citizens are now looking for ANY man ANY WHERE that wears a size 10 to 11 tennis shoe.

It is evident that NOW is the time to bring in the outside experience and expertise offered to the Task Force early on in this investigation by numerous individuals highly trained and qualified in dealing with serial killers, such as Robert Keppel.

The Citizens of this community have heard on numerous occasions from the Task Force that it is pleased with the course of the investigation.[33]

At this point, the newsletter quotes from various media reports published since 2002 that were basically supportive or even laudatory of the work of the Task Force. Then, the memo shifts to the concern of citizens about the amount of money being allocated to the search for the serial killer:

We know there are hundreds of rape kits still needing to be tested along with over one thousand swabs taken by the Task Force during the course of this investigation. It is a time consuming and expensive process.

The Governor has stated that money is no object. Since there is a huge backlog of testing that needs to be completed, C.A.S.K. suggests the Task Force ferret out this work either to other crime labs or private labs located throughout the country. This will speed the process and greatly enhance the probability that the serial killer will be caught before another woman is brutally murdered.

Also, there is not a picture, in the traditional sense, of the serial killer. Maybe it is time for the Baton Rouge Task Force to be progressive in its search. Do something never done before. The Task Force has enough information that it can build an "internal" picture of the serial killer. Things he can not change. Things that are constant. This would be a challenge in the sense that the Citizens would have to look hard at those closest to them.

It was reported early on in the newspapers that the victims were sexually assaulted. The serial killer can then logically assume that the DNA connection is from his sperm, from which much can be determined about an individual. Footprints were obtained at two separate crime scenes, one of those being in mud.

What is his estimated height and weight?

How does he walk? Does he walk on the inside of his feet? Does he have a limp? Does he favor one leg?

What is his blood type?

Is he sterile or fertile?

Does he have any known illness or disease?

In describing the above characteristics, the Task Force may motivate an individual to question the activities of someone he/she knows. At the same time this information may enable an individual to rule out someone he/she may suspect, thereby cutting down on the waste of crucial time spent by the Task Force investigating false leads.

If the Task Force decides it is not possible for what ever reason to determine or release the above information the Citizens would like a detailed explanation as to why. We do not request details about the evidence obtained, because it stands to reason that some things do indeed need to be held back.

In summary, C.A.S.K. credits the Task Force for the hard work and dedication they have shown to bringing this animal to justice. However, C.A.S.K. believes it is now time to bring in the experts that have offered their extensive experience and wealth of knowledge to this investigation, send some of the DNA swabs obtained from this case and rape kits to various labs throughout the country in order to speed the progress of this investigation, and help us narrow our search for the serial killer by painting us a picture we can use.

Thank you,

C.A.S.K.

PO Box 78398

Baton Rouge, Louisiana 70837[34]

The memo concludes with a promotion of some of the group's upcoming events.[35]

Meanwhile, even more pressure was being put on the Task Force by a petition drive that was started by relatives of the slain victims. It called for the Governor to make changes in the top ranks of the Task Force and also requested more manpower, twenty additional men, be hired and devoted to the investigation into the identified victims of the serial killer, Green, Pace, Kinamore, Colomb, and Yoder. Responding to the petition, the Governor said:

Absolutely I'll talk to anybody and I just want people to be understood we know it's frustrating but we're not gonna hold this thing back on a monetary basis.[36]

As it turned out, changes in the FBI that would affect the Task Force were already under way. Special Agent Ken Kaiser who headed up the Louisiana division had been transferred to Boston, replaced by Louis Reigal III from FBI headquarters in Washington. This change was to be made in June.[37]

Yet another rally was held at LSU on March 26. More than 300 students and faculty members gathered to learn whatever new information they could learn about the case, spending their free time and time they should have been in class to hear from those close to the investigation of the serial killer. The message directed to the wall of women in the audience was the chilling reality that they are not so different from the five women known to have been murdered by the serial killer. Lisa of CASK said: "None of these women did anything to provoke this killer. They simply caught his attention just as you could." One LSU student who attended the rally said, "I'm tired of being scared and I'm tired of constantly looking over my shoulder. I don't like feeling that way."[38]

Some theorized the serial killer strikes around holidays or other momentous occasions. With the Easter holiday approaching, Lynne Marino, mother of Pam Kinamore, the serial killer's third known victim sent out a warning to all females: "On a beautiful day like today, I hate to be the one to tell you, but Easter is coming up and this guy has probably already picked out his next victim. Don't let your guard down and don't let this man take another life."[39]

Also present at the rally was LSU Chancellor Mark Emmert. Emmert said that LSU added extra security patrol and cameras around the university to protect both its students and the Baton Rouge community.[40]

Among those in the crowd was Sterling Colomb whose sister Dene', is the killer's fourth known victim. "I'm here for support. My sister is dead and gone and if there is something that I can do to prevent another person from dying I'm there," said Colomb.[41]

In a rare defense of the Baton Rouge Police and the Serial Killer Task Force, Ann Pace the mother of Murray Pace reminded everyone that police are doing everything they can to not jeopardize the case. She explained authorities have their reasons for not disclosing much of the information and details on the case.[42]

Aside from warnings, the rally focused on self-defense and safety techniques. Investigators were also on hand questioning students about suspicious activity in the area. LSU police said they have received 50 calls this year regarding suspicious persons. They said 34 of those calls came in March, 2003 after DNA connected Carrie Yoder's murder to the serial killer.[43]

An LSU program called STAY SAFE was launched on April 10, and by doing so, the school was taking the student safety issues seriously and were vowing to make student safety its top priority. Students, faculty and staff filed into the new academic center at the school to learn what they could about how to better protect themselves on campus. One student in attendance said, "I actually had a class and my professor let us all come to the class because he felt that it was going to be important for us." Other students said they were glad the Chancellor and LSU police took time to talk with them. However, the person they were especially happy to hear from was Lee Stanton, the boyfriend of Carrie Yoder. Students said that Stanton's message hit home. "He said Carrie Yoder didn't have a set pattern and that she was cautious and I don't think a lot of people realize that."[44] Students added that Stanton said the reason Carrie was extremely cautious was because she lived alone and she fit the victim profile. Stanton made a service announcement for LSU students talking about Carrie and what everyone should learn from her death.[45]

Speakers at the April 10 rally used the occasion to announce that LSU was in the process of safeguarding its campus. Campus police said they had identified 17 additional locations for call boxes to be installed. They told students to look for blue marker lights highlighting every phone on campus in the near future. Governor Mike Foster, though not in attendance, did what he could to get into the act. A speaker announced that within the past week Foster had made an additional $250,000 available to LSU to hire more patrol officers and put extra security cameras and lights on the campus.[46]

A final rally before the apprehension of the serial killer was the Justice For All Rally, which was dedicated to the memory of Charlotte Murray Pace. The May 18th rally was held 13 days before the one year anniversary of Pace's murder. This rally was also the first attended by the parents of Carrie Yoder.[47]

The rally was an emotionally powerful reminder for the city to be on guard, and was perhaps the most emotional Baton Rouge rally to date. CASK had one cross for every woman victim of an unsolved murder. "Oh my God, look how many women have died," said Lynne Marino. "How can anybody look at those crosses and not turn this guy in if they know him." "It's so powerful to look at that (the crosses). I was emotionally overwhelmed to see that," said Ann Pace. "I couldn't imagine we could get to here, yet here we are." Pace says she got here on Murray's strength. "We always said she was born saying I will not and you can't make me and we draw from that spirit to get through today and tomorrow and the next day. I mean we're working for Murray, we're her team," said Ann Pace.[48]

"Pam will be dead one year July the 12th and I won't be able to say last year she was here, last year we did this, last year we did that. That's really hard," said Lynne Marino.[49]

Dave Yoder's daughter, Carrie Lynn became the serial killer's fifth victim and is the most recent. "It's difficult circumstances to be here but we felt it was important," said Dave Yoder. "Everyone is at a different stage in this process. It's only been 10, 11 weeks for us so the folks that have been at this for a year and a half are at a totally different stage of grieving."[50]

The polished professional Louis Cataldie, who had to separate and compartmentalize his personal feelings from his professional judgments in the case from the beginning, was not emotionally prepared for what happened at the rally. By his own admission, he was just not ready for the bell that tolled once for each of the confirmed or suspected victims of the serial killer.[51]

Along with the proliferation of rallies in Baton Rouge there was a proliferation of rumors and even some urban legends about the serial killer, just about all of which turned out to be false. A poster known as LAP posted this memo which everyone in the city would have been glad to read. In a message titled "Got Him," the writer said:

They got him.
It was a professor at the University.
His wife turned him in.
One of his sons used to date Colomb.
More later I guess.
What did they say in the news conference?

LAP[52]

This rumor, like scores of others churning in Baton Rouge, was totally untrue.

The news conference that is mentioned in this posting is the one held in late March, 2003. This day was memorable because it was announced to the public that citizens should consider more races than the white man that people had been looking for for months. Also the public was asked to look beyond the "white truck" that had been suspected as the vehicle that the killer had used to transport his victims.[53] It is hard to imagine the anger level escalating beyond the level that had been present in Baton Rouge, but the messages posted in Dr. Godwin's group were just that, a torrent of diatribes against the Task Force. Check out the tone of this message:

The public is being asked to "broaden our thinking about this offender" per Mary Ann Godawa.

I would like to see the TF "broaden their thinking"!

The Yoder investigation has uncovered some "critical information"! GREAT; this is good news!

They do NOT want us to rely on the sketch of a white male, but to look at the possibility that the SK may be dark skinned, black, or mixed heritage/inter-racial. UH-OH! Interesting!

Sounds like they might be "crawfishing" (Dr. G. down here that means backing up when you might have made a mistake!)

Note: The FBI profile NEVER stated the race of the BRSK, however, they have been verbally saying white male for sometime now. Sounds like they may have a lead on someone who is not white or could be white, but have dark skin coloring!??? The person of interest sketch "may have had a legitimate reason to be in the area" and he has not been identified as a suspect in the case. This is where the sketch originated (in the area where the Colomb body dump took place.) My understanding is that MANY tips have been given of people who do NOT resemble the sketch.

The truck description should not limit tips; the SK could own or use other vehicles (Duh!) Evidently the white truck theory is not working; nevertheless, if I am correct, the majority of the DNA swabbing included those in white trucks BECAUSE THE TF DECIDED TO SWAB THOSE PEOPLE FIRST! Sounds like more "crawfishing to me"! The white truck theory came up from the HYPNOTIZED witness that saw a nude woman at 3 a.m. exiting Whiskey Bay the morning after Kinamore was abducted. The truck theory was reinforced when a white truck was seen behind Colomb's car. I welcome feedback and would like to get YOUR take on this; please, everyone jump in! There appears to be something definitely up with the holding of this press conference! Either they have a suspect, have a witness who has seen someone who is not 'light skinned', etc. That could mean he is italian, black, oriental, hispanic, indian, a mix (which is very prominent in Louisiana), or some other 'foreign' person, etc.

Take care, Leslie[54]

The public was becoming distressed as well, judging from the following news story that was posted to Dr. Godwin's discussion group. Entitled, "Serial killer clues going undetected, activists fear; They urge quick DNA tests on older crimes," the story was posted to Dr. Godwin's discussion group on Wednesday March 26, 2003.[55]

Arguing that the serial killer might have committed previous crimes, CASK was urging officials, as it had done in its newsletter, to speed DNA testing on thousands of pieces of violent-crime-scene and sexual-assault evidence backlogged at the state crime lab. "This guy's DNA could be sitting in a rape kit waiting to be tested," said Stormy of CASK. "We could have a rape victim out there who can give us a better description of this guy."[56]

In 2001, the state crime lab began DNA testing on evidence from violent crimes and sexual assaults throughout the state, said Captain Brian Wynne, crime lab director. Since then, the lab has received requests to test evidence in more than 1,400 cases, which can have one to five samples of biological material that need analysis. As of the week of March 26, the crime lab has completed DNA testing on 435 of those cases, Wynne said. "It's a very time-consuming process."[57]

Wynne said he expected the lab, which has four DNA analysts, to double its testing speed after another five DNA analysts completed their training and begin working in the spring of 2003. Six more DNA analysts will be added later in 2003 or early in 2004. The new employees will fill the nine vacancies that have vacancies that have existed in the lab's DNA testing program since its inception in April 2001 and another two vacancies created by recent resignations. "It's very difficult to fill the positions," he said. Of the 11 new employees, five were hired July 1, three were hired in November, and three will be hired soon, meaning, in the spring of 2003.[58]

In addition to the 1,400 cases of crime-scene evidence, the state crime lab had received requests to test more than 1,200 saliva swabs of men from the Baton Rouge and Lafayette areas as part of the serial killer investigation. Wynne declined to comment about how many of the swabs have been DNA-tested. Baton Rouge police Corporal Mary Ann Godawa, a spokeswoman for the multi-agency Task Force, confirmed that more tests need to be performed but declined to say how many.[59]

Since the fall of 2002 the Task Force had obtained swabs from neighbors, friends, boyfriends, relatives, co-workers and acquaintances of the five women linked to the serial killer by DNA. Suspicious people identified by citizens and the Task Force also have been swabbed. "If it's something we feel is urgent, (the crime lab) will turn it around for us quickly," Godawa said. "They've bent over backwards for us." She said that when the "level of caution" is not as high for a particular test, the wait for its results are longer. She said she could not provide the specific lengths of time the tests have taken.[60]

According to the FBI profile of the killer, "he has likely been involved in any or all of the following: domestic abuse, workplace violence, random assaultive behavior, threatening behavior." The FBI profile also says the killer probably has come to "the attention of law enforcement in the past, even if for seemingly minor offenses, including trespassing, breaking and entering, and peeping."[61]

Jack Levin, director of Brudnick Center on Violence and Conflict at Northeastern University in Boston and the author of several books on serial killers, said most of them do not graduate to murder from lesser crimes, but "there are important exceptions." "We're talking about the odds," Levin said. "The odds are he does not have a criminal record. . . . But you've got to work at that possibility (that he does) until it's eliminated."[62]

CASK members, echoing sentiments expressed in their newsletter, said they would like to see more money spent clearing the backlog of evidence testing at the crime lab. Earlier, Governor Foster said money would be "no object" in the investigation. However, Foster had not recently received requests from the Task Force for more money to help speed the testing, according to spokesman Steven Johnston. The group is urging officials to outsource the work to another public or private lab if the state crime lab cannot quickly complete the job. A CASK member identified as Stormy said: "It's imperative we get them out and get them tested so we can increase the speed of the investigation." "That would increase the possibility that we catch this guy before he brutally murders another woman."[63] Wynne said he plans to ask the Legislature this month (March, 2003) for an extra $400,000 for more DNA analysis equipment and supplies.

It is the crime lab's first request for extra money prompted by the needs of the serial killer task force. Wynne said he did not request more money, equipment or personnel before because the lab's resources were "sufficient" to handle the workload presented by the ongoing investigation. Godawa echoed that, saying the task force has been satisfied with the rate at which the crime lab returns test results. "They have been working very hard," she said.[64]

New theories came to light during this time when there was a waiting game being played in which the public was waiting for the DNA evidence to analyzed and the serial killer appeared to be biding his time in choosing his next victim. One of these theories was the "cell phone theory." This theory first emerged after Gina Green's cell phone had been found near a business called Ready Portions Meat. This business was closely monitored and investigated by members of the group, some even visiting the place to look it over and to ask questions of some of the employees.[65] After a period of dormancy the theory re-emerged as some members of the group found a cell phone connection between some of the cases:

Does the removal of cell or cordless phones have any relevance to unforced entry? Hypothetically speaking, of the five murders linked by DNA, there are two which logical explanation for unforced entry are evident.

1. Kinamore, left keys in door
2. Colomb, abducted from roadside

Of the three cases that are left, what is the common denominator?

1. Green, cell phone initially missing, but later found
2. Pace, cordless hand phone still missing

Could it be that the SK is simply asking his victims to use their phones to make a call bc he is stranded, etc. That would explain why there are no forced entries and why phones are missing. But that leads to the Yoder case. No phone missing to "our knowledge". According to experts, SK's become more refined in their killings. Could it be that with Yoder he struck before she retrieved the phone.

Also...although these crimes HAVEN'T been linked to the case what about Moore and DeSoto??? Moore: abducted while jogging (needs an "unforced entry" explanation). BUT, what about Desoto???? DeSoto: cordless hand phone still missing. HHHmmmm....just something to ponder?!?!?!?!?!?![66]

This post and others like it eventually led members of the group to closely scrutinize the areas where police had located cell phones and the possible uses that the serial killer may have made of such phones. Are these merely "trophies" or indicative of a clever ploy used as the killer mode of operation?[67]

The information released at the March 21 press conference also caused members of the group to rethink certain suspects who had aroused suspicion but who were basically eliminated because they were not white or were driving a vehicle other than a white truck. The following post was the beginning of the "Pathfinder Theory." When someone pointed out that there had been reports of someone in a white Pathfinder near Yoder's apartment, alarms went off within the group:

Good lord, Sandi!!!!!!!!!!!!!!! This guy was also in a white pathfinder that was reported by SEVERAL people as sitting near Carrie's home! In fact, one night there were police CHASING a white pathfinder on Airline Highway (I think that was the location) and a friend of mine called to say she was wondering if it was related to all the reports of a guy sitting outside/near Carrie's home!!!!!!! What the heck has been going on? I do NOT know how many white pathfinders there are in Louisiana, but I definitely do not think they would be as prevalent as a white truck! Now, just speculating here......IF this is all true about the guy sitting outside of the home and NO ONE called (they were wrong and could have possibly stopped Carrie from being killed).

NOTE: I DO SAY POSSIBLE!!?? Sometimes I do think I am living in some kind of Alfred Hitchcock movie the more I hear! Take care and be safe and vigilant!!!!!!! Leslie[68]

Another member of the group weighed in:

I didn't know that about Carrie Yoder (a dark complicated man being seen near her house). This only confirms to me that the LE isn't putting pieces of the puzzle together. If the man that I had reported is similar to the description of the man that was near Carries'....wouldn't the LE be some what curious? Or concerned? It also makes me wonder how many of the tips they actually view. Or if the people taking the calls make the judgments on which calls THEY think are important. Someone had asked what he was driving--an older (white) pathfinder or rodeo with black trim and a tire on the back. I tried to get the license number, but I couldn't find it! The incident happened on Foster Drive, in front of the School Board. I clocked the mileage to (near) Carries house and it's approx. 5 miles (give or take) he headed in that direction.[69]

Others were more consumed by the issue of race; many potential suspects had been eliminated due to the racial issue. In fact, the Task Force had some early information about Lee but chose to ignore it because he was Black. Many were now forced to go back through their recollections and think about instances where Black suspects had been subjects of potential interest. That had happened early on in the case when people living near Carrie Yoder's apartment had seen a suspicious looking Black man hanging out in the neighborhood in the days prior to Carrie's disappearance.[70]

While the public waited and continued to form their own theories about the serial killer, Baton Rouge Police Chief Pat Englade was increasingly the target of criticism and anger. As the press reported, the man leading the hunt for the serial killer had become the lightning rod for much of the frustration and criticism of an edgy public fearing another victim. Englade was being accused of hiding information that could keep the public safe and being unable to handle the depth of an investigation required to track the man who murdered at least five women in Baton Rouge and Lafayette.[71]

The demands of the case had been such that Englade could not leave the case at work. People approached him in stores, contacted him by e-mail and phoned his wife with tips and scraps of information they thought and hoped might finger the killer. "It's very difficult for me to go out in public right now. I can't go out to Wal-Mart without six or seven people coming up to me," Englade told reporters. He works nights, weekends, and holidays, checking in on his computer when he gets home at night. He tried to make it to as many of his son's high school basketball games as possible, but even on days off, he phoned in to the Task Force of officials working on the case. "I've aged about 10 years in the last nine months. You never leave this situation whether you want a few hours sleep or want to go to dinner with your wife," he said.[72]

Chief of Police since 2001 and a police officer with the department since 1973, Englade was less than a year into that job when the serial killer murdered his first victim. The intense public scrutiny didn't arise until the third murder was linked in the summer of 2002. Since then, the media and public interest spotlights have focused on the man with the gray flattop haircut and glasses who wasn't used to the barrage of cameras that have become the norm. "I don't know if anybody, maybe except the White House, deals with the media onslaught we've had to deal with in the past few months," Englade said. "We've had some growing pains. We've made some mistakes, I admit it."[73]

At the top of the list, he wonders if the daily media briefings aired live on local TV over the summer of 2002 were a wise idea. Often, police had no new information to offer, and the briefings became a monotonous reiteration of past details. The briefings stopped, but the complaints continued. Some people say Englade is too brusque, seems defensive and doesn't handle intense questioning well. Few question his dedication to finding the killer, but they question whether he has given people enough information to protect themselves. "I think the public is intelligent and they want to know what's going on without it jeopardizing or impeding the investigation," said Yvonne Welch, the Baton Rouge legislator who represents the area near LSU where several of the victims lived. Geri Teasley, who organizes the monthly rallies to remember the serial killer victims and other women whose murders remain unsolved, said the public feels alienated by Englade and the other authorities working on the case. "He could very well be talking to the next victim. I think that hasn't necessarily hit him yet," said Lisa of CASK."[74]

Englade said he's given out as much information as he could and wonders if he's provided tidbits that ultimately shut down trails to investigate, like the type of shoe print the killer left behind at crime scenes and the description of a white truck that might be connected to the killer. "You put them on the scale and try to balance them out," he said. "I think we give out the information we think is important to the public, without endangering the case."[75]

Englade said the criticism is unfair, but he understands people are frustrated and afraid. He's not always even-tempered, though, getting visibly frustrated by the attitude of some women who he believes aren't doing enough to protect themselves. "I don't know what else we can do to hammer this home. You've got to lock your doors. You have to take care of yourself. We cannot put a policeman in everybody's house," Englade told women, his voice rising, at a March campus forum at LSU.[76]

Women worry those outbursts from Englade hint at a case he can't solve, pointing to statements made that police "are learning as they go." Cries have been loud for bringing in outside assistance. The FBI, state police and several other agencies are in the Task Force, but many people want police consulting everyone who's ever dealt with a serial killer investigation or researched DNA evidence.[77] Dr. Godwin eventually had "backdoor" discussions with Task Force members but they were unproductive.

Governor Mike Foster, the mayor and other officials in Baton Rouge have said they have complete confidence in Englade's ability to lead the task force and find the killer. Foster said he visits the task force once a week to check on them. "If this guy makes one mistake, they've got him," Foster has said of the task force and Englade's leadership. "They're that professional. They're that good."[78] Englade said he's talked to experts all over the world, including former law enforcement officers, investigators in serial killer cases and DNA researchers. "I don't have a photo, even though some people think I do, of this person in my back pocket," he said.[79]

As much as Louisianans wanted to believe its public officials and to have faith in them, the state has a long history full of reasons not to. As John Fund of the *Wall Street Journal* described the situation: "In just the past generation, the Pelican State has had a governor, an attorney general, three successive insurance commissioners, a congressman, a federal judge, a state Senate president and a swarm of local officials convicted."[80] Recent history bore no reason for optimism, either.[81] With a record like this, there's no question that citizens had little faith in government and I'm sure the serial killer case just added to this culture of activism in the absence of official action.

A significant breakthrough in the case occurred when the Task Force, now casting a wider suspect net by looking at cases involving Black suspects, revealed some recent unusual activity going on in St. Martin's Parish. The press conference to announce these developments was transmitted to the group as it was happening by one very active and concerned member, Leslie Davis. In a message entitled "Press Conference: What I Am Hearing," the group learned the following information on Friday, May 23, 2003. This might be called "the St. Martin's breakthrough."

I AM GIVING A RENDITION OF WHAT I JUST HEARD ON THE PRESS CONFERENCE: I AM TYPING AS I LISTEN TO THE PRESS CONFERENCE SO HOPEFULLY THIS IS ACCURATE AND MY 85 WPM WILL HELP HERE..........

3 specific incidents in St. Martin Parish

Offender approached in a "rouse" approach. Approach used by offender using a story to disarm the victim in order to minimize any red flags.

Very good looking light skin blacked male
Personable and disarmingly charming
Non-threatening, smooth
Muscular, short hair and clean shaven
Good looking, good teeth and skin
20's to 30's age
1997 Mitsubishi Mirage = gold damage/front/rear bumper
License plates says Hampton on the front
Investigating three cases of a man using a "ruse" to get into the homes of these women.

1st incident:

Offender asked to use a phone and phone book to look up someone who I am doing work for because I can't locate them. He was looking inside the home while standing on the porch. Asked if her husband was home. Very nice skin. Occurred during late morning.

2nd incident:

Similar offender
Approached woman in trailer home
Looking for a "john smith" = looked around the home
Asked about relationship to photos on the wall
Was asking for phone/phone book
Is husband here? he asked

3rd incident:

Pulled truck behind a woman leaving a large retail store
Extended his hand/showed sign of warmth and friendliness
Introduced himself as "Anthony"
Friendly and disarming
When she pulled her hand back and she looked, she observed him, mas-
turbating in his car as he pulled her toward him (I think while he was
clasping her hand).
Described also as smooth skin/good looking

Overview:

Offender using different first names and various modified "ruses."

A profile has been compiled/here are parts of what they read:

Very likely he approached women in their home but was interrupted
when someone came to the door also (man, dog, child, etc.)

Opinion that offender is spending great deal of time watching and ob-
serving woman; if he makes an approach it could be from masturbating
in public, following these women or using a "ruse" with women.

At the time it may have seemed harmless to women, including
women in Baton Rouge.

Offender has been seen in several different vehicles

May have borrowed cars or used various vehicles from work, etc.

Any information about the suspect call 389-3310.

Q&A:

Is there a sketch to be made available?
Yes! To be released at the end of the press conference

Any DNA recovered?
Information that there has not been conclusive evidence to link to the SK.

What is timeline?
Within a 30-45 day period; info was aired about suspect

Actual assaults?

Yes, no details given.

What are descriptions of victims?

Not all brunettes

Any relation between victims such as age, etc.?

Range in different ages; no specific age group.

All victims race?

All black

Reporter asking for a picture of the sketch to be held up?
Seem to be avoiding the question and saying they will hand it out AF-TER the press conference

What about original POI?

Still wanting to question the original person of interest.

Full coverage at 5, 6, and 10 p.m.
TV went back to regular broadcasting

Take care, Leslie[82]

The man being described at the press conference, as Leslie frantically typed to keep up with the information, was Derrick Todd Lee.

There was a measure of justice in the serial killer case when the person who revealed Lee's capture to Dr. Godwin's discussion group was none other than the cousin of Carrie Lynn Yoder. On Tuesday, May 27, 2003 at 9:30 P.M., Steve Yoder announced to the group:

The gig is up. Picked up within the last hour or so in Atlanta. From the family of one of the victims, I can now say thank you to the many of you who have, in your own way, helped bring this stage to a conclusion. I have monitored this message board since March 3, 2003 and think that Dr. Godwin has provided an incredible public service in moderating this board and those of you who have participated have helped keep the level of awareness at a peak level since my cousin Carrie was murdered. Our family could ask for nothing more.

The missteps along the way by law enforcement are obvious and expected. No one knows exactly how to handle these situations until you are in them and hindsight is always 20-20. Before you begin slamming them for being incompetent, understand that I've gotten to know many of these men and women personally and can tell you that our family is appreciative of their efforts. Focus your rage on Derrick Lee....not the people who have devoted a great deal of energy at the expense of personal sacrifice in their own lives to find this pathetic creep.

Derrick Lee is a monster who should have been off the streets a long time ago....long before anyone heard of Gina Green, Murray Pace, Pam Kinamore, Dene' Colomb or my cousin Carrie ... let's work together to make certain no one else suffers at his hands.

Best to all of you....

Steve Yoder[83]

About a week later, one of the members of the group pointed out that the work on the serial killer case was not yet finished, though Steve Yoder's emotional memo had already begun to speak of the case in the past tense. There were still more than 70 unsolved murders in south Louisiana, and this led a poster known as "snettles2001" began to wonder if the necessary work would ever be carried forward. In a memo titled "More Work To Be Done: Would It Be?" snettles2001 wrote:

82 Unsolved Murders

Praying that these 82 murders will someday be solved. Please feel free to add or make corrections. One thing that I noticed while researching this list of victims names was that I could find no unsolved murders for the year 1993.

1981
Eleanor Parker

1985
Melissa Montz

1988
Charlotte L Sauerwin

1990
Tammy Bowers
Jeannie LaVigne

1992
Gloria Stanford
Joyce Taylor
Connie Warner

1994
Detra Adams
Ann Bryan
April Daigre
Debra Ann Haselden
Griezelda Griffin Jones
Jippari Salters

1995
Christina Daigle
Cynthia Green
Deborah Hunt
Patricia Ann Jackson
Lakisha Richardson

1996
Angela Arnold
Patricia Carter
Terry Jackson
Rosalyn Rankins
Jackie Lynn Smith

1997
Eugenie Boisfontaine
Tina Capers
Shannon Shelvin
Diana Marie Williams

1998
Elizabeth Deville
Randi Mebruer
Janice Stokes
Claretha Thomas

1999
Elizabeth Darensbourg
Florida Edwards
Kassie Federer
Katherine Hall
Shirley Mikell

Lisa Pate
Pamela Patin
Hardee Schmidt
Gloria Tanner
Danielle Thibodeaux
Muoi Voung

2000
Ingrid Breeland
Veronica Courtney
Priscilla Durden
Monique Edwards
Robin Gremillion
Patricia Hawkins
Patricia Martin
Marilyn Nevils
Lillian Robinson
Jessica Walker
Sondra Kathy Walker
Tannis Walker
Dianna Williams
Joyce Williams

2001
Damitra Augustus
Keisha Bradley
Sylvia Cobb
Gina Wilson Green
Cennea Guidry
Monica Morgan

2002
Frances Baldwin
Letha Bowie
Alicia Carver
Lora Causey
Dene Colomb
Geralyn DeSoto
Mari Ann Fowler
Teresa Gilcrease
Tawanda Renee' Hayes
Pam Kinamore
Barbara Ann Lacour
Rebecca Miller
Christina Moore

Charotte Murray Pace
Rene Newman

2003
Mona Burt
Antoinette Dunn
Linda Krummel
Carrie Lynn Yoder[84]

Even months before Lee was captured, one member of the group wondered what would happen when it was all over:

With all this time and effort being put into tracking this person, bringing him in and putting him away, I wonder...

I wonder what everyone that is SO involved in this is going to do when it is over....? Will the victims simply become statistics?

Will everyone's vigilance be replaced with complacence?

Is this community going to wait for another crime spree before taking action?

What? What are you going to do?

How about you Dr. G? Will you continue this list no matter how much of a decline in its use?[85]

Dr. Godwin was on his way to Baton Rouge to confront the Task Force with new information about the serial killer but instead spent a good deal of time trying to learn whatever he could about Derrick Lee. Afterward, he wrote this message of appreciation to the group:

I was interviewed several times by the media during my visit to Baton Rouge. However, I have no evidence that any of the interviews were ever shown.

I really enjoyed my trip to Baton Rouge. Leslie was terrific and so were all the people that I meet especially those who helped me obtain quick info on Derrick Lee. I also enjoyed my trip to New Orleans.

Thanks to all who supported my trip; your help is greatly appreciated.[86]

A few days earlier, Godwin had emphasized, "The timing of the TF decision to release the information about the suspect Lee is directly related to my visit to Baton Rouge.[87] However, no sooner had Dr. Godwin gotten back to North Carolina than he came to realize that outside consultants were no longer needed in the case. This was clear from his failure to get any television time in the wake of Derrick Lee's capture and arrest. In a fast moving, media driven postmodern world, the press was already closing the books on the serial killer case, at least the "in search of" stage. Now, Derrick Todd Lee was in the spotlight.

ENDNOTES

1. Posted March 13, 2003.

2. "Yoder's Body Recovered." *Baton Rouge Advocate*, March 14, 2003.

3. Cataldie, *ibid.*

4. Posted March 17, 2003.

5. Posted March 14, 2003.

6. Posted April 7, 2003.

7. Cataldie, *ibid.*

8. Posted March 15, 2003.

9. Posted March 24, 2003.

10. Posted May 20, 2003.

11. Posted May 20, 2003.

12. Posted March 20, 2005.

13. Posted March 17, 2003.

14. *Ibid.*

15. *Ibid.*

16. *Ibid.*

17. *Ibid.*

18. *Ibid.*

19. *Ibid.*

20. Posted March 18, 2003.

21. Stephanie A. Stanley, "BR Women Convert Anger to Action." *New Orleans Times Picayune*, March 18, 2003; posted March 18, 2003.

22. *Ibid.*

23. *Ibid.*

24. *Ibid.*

25. *Ibid.*

26. "Serial Killer Fear Causes Increase in Baton Rouge Gun Sales." Posted March 19, 2003.

27. Cataldie, *ibid.*

28. "Serial Killer Fear ...." Posted March 19, 2003.

29. *Ibid.*

30. Posted March 18, 2003.

31. Posted March 18, 2003.

32. Posted March 23, 2003.

33. Posted March 24, 2003.

34. *Ibid.*

35. *Ibid.*

36. Posted March 27, 2003.

37. *Ibid.*

38. "LSU Rally Advises Women To Remain Alert of Serial Killer." Posted March 27, 2003.

39. *Ibid.*

40. *Ibid.*

41. *Ibid.*

42. *Ibid.*

43. *Ibid.*

44. "LSU Launches 'Stay Safe' Campaign." Posted April 10, 2003.

45. *Ibid.*

46. *Ibid.*

47. "Justice For All Rally." Posted May 18, 2003.

48. *Ibid.*

49. *Ibid.*

50. *Ibid.*

51. Cataldie, *ibid.*

52. Posted March 21, 2003.

53. Posted March 23, 2003.

54. Posted March 23, 2003.

55. Posted March 26, 2003.

56. *Ibid.*

57. *Ibid.*

58. *Ibid.*

59. *Ibid.*

60. *Ibid.*

61. *Ibid.*

62. *Ibid.*

63. *Ibid.*

64. *Ibid.*

65. These messages were posted on or around May 1, 2003.

66. Posted May 13, 2003.

67. These messages were posted on or around May 1, 2003.

68. Posted May 17, 2003.

69. Posted May 17, 2003.

70. Godwin, *ibid.*

71. Posted May 17, 2003.

72. *Ibid.*

73. *Ibid.*

74. *Ibid.*

75. *Ibid.*

76. *Ibid.*

77. *Ibid.*

78. *Ibid.*

79. *Ibid.*

80. John Fund, "A Swamp of Corruption: In Katrina's Wake, Louisiana's Political Culture Needs A Cleanup Too." *Jewish World Review*, September 25, 2005.

81. *Ibid.*

82. Posted May 23, 2003.

83. Posted May 27, 2003.

84. Posted June 2, 2003.

85. Posted April 6, 2003.

86. Posted May 29, 2003.

87. Posted May 27, 2003.

Chapter 6

The Arrest and Trial of Derrick Todd Lee

The same day that Derrick Todd Lee was swabbed by local officials in St. Francisville, Lee's wife Jacqueline suddenly took their young son and daughter from school, claiming that the family was moving to Los Angeles. The couple then quickly packed up their belongings and abandoned their brown-brick ranch style house at 4273 U.S. 61 in St. Francisville in West Feliciana Parish, Louisiana.[1]

On May 27, 2003 Atlanta police working with a joint FBI-metropolitan Atlanta task force apprehended Lee at a hotel where he was lodging.[2] He had become a hero of sorts to many who lived there as permanent residents, doing errands for them, conducting Bible studies, holding barbeques, and romancing several of the women. Residents there found it hard to believe that the smooth, personable young man they met was wanted as the suspect in the Baton Rouge serial killings. Lee was observed poking around a tire store in suburban Atlanta before police caught up with him at his hotel. He was arrested without a struggle.[3]

Lee waived extradition and was flown back to Louisiana the following day. Initially he was charged with only Carrie Lynn Yoder's murder. However, by early June he was also accused of the rape and murder of Green, Pace, Kinamore and Colomb based on DNA evidence linking him to the crimes.[4]

After Lee had been taken into police custody, the police with the help of the FBI immediately were focusing on trying to locate his estranged wife Jacqueline and the couple's two children. It was hoped that Jacqueline might be able to provide clues into Lee's behavior and whereabouts during the crimes. Family members suspected she was hiding out of fear.[5] This was confirmed by a Baton Rouge news reporter who wrote that family members of Jacqueline Lee claimed that "she lived in denial of her husband's transgressions, which include stalking, peeping into windows and infidelity."[6] According to another newsman familiar with the case, Jacqueline's aunt claimed she was afraid of her husband and at one point against her wishes he had a mistress move into their home.[7]

Initially, Jacqueline and the couple's two children could not be traced. But by June the FBI located the three in Chicago, where Lee had fled immediately after leaving Louisiana. Investigators were interested in Jacqueline not only for questioning purposes but also because they needed her consent before they could begin digging (for victims) on the property of her former residence.[8]

Meanwhile, on Dr. Godwin's discussion group, the number of messages dropped from a high of 1,794 in May, 2003 to 1,182 the next month; this was followed by a precipitous decline to only 94 messages posted in July, 2003. This trend indicated, first of all, that interest in the case among the discussion group's members had virtually vanished, or that the attention of the members had gone elsewhere. There was some residual interest in the Lee case, such as when it was going to go to trial, and what the outcome might be.[9] A few messages tried to keep morale up and to keep women on the alert since there was very likely to be more serial killers given the large number of women missing; and it was also known due to some research by Dr. Godwin that Derrick Lee was in custody during 2000 when many women came up missing.[10] The following is representative of these "keep on the alert" kinds of memos:

> Believe me, Dr. Godwin, the criminal element is STILL out there. If my memory serves me correctly, within a week of Derrick Todd Lee's capture, there was a woman who was almost abducted in a shopping center parking area in Lafayette. We must forever stay alert and on guard.
>
> In other words, STILL PAY ATTENTION AND TAKE HEED LADIES!![11]

There did not appear to be much interest at all in following up the evidence in any of the other cases of missing women, except for those linked to the Zachary cases, and these would eventually become linked to Lee. Nor was there much interest in following up on potential victims of Sean Vincent Gillis, the second Baton Rouge serial killer identified by police in 2004 and later convicted for multiple murders. Only 120 messages were posted during the entire year of 2004.[12]

During the investigation into Lee, the police learned that he had an extensive criminal history. Lee's youthful record included a string of juvenile offenses that stretched back to 1984 when he was caught peeping into the home of a St. Francisville woman. It would mark the first of many such offenses, and investigators would learn that Lee never outgrew his teenage fetish.[13]

As Lee grew older his "rap sheet" became more extended, including arrests for attempted first-degree murder, stalking, peeping into homes, as well as break in and burglary, among other crimes. That the serial killer might have a record for some petty crimes is something that Dr. Godwin had suspected even from his earliest days in tracking the Baton Rouge case.[14] According to press accounts of Lee's arrests and related incidents, the information below represents the documented activity of Lee between 1992 and 2001 that was reported to the media.[15]

In November 1992, Lee was arrested for illegal entry and burglary of Zachary resident Rob Benge's house. The following January, Lee and an accomplice, Thomas Whitaker Jr. were arrested for breaking into the home of seventy-three-year old Melvin Foster, whom they beat with a stick and robbed. Then in July, 1993, Lee was sentenced to one year in prison for burglary.[16] During 1993, there were no women reported missing in Baton Rouge.

In September, 1995, Lee was arrested for a peeping incident and resisting arrest, after being chased and caught by police after looking into the window of a Lake Charles woman. During the same month, Lee was arrested again for stealing from a Salvation Army Thrift Store.[17]

It would be about two years before Lee was caught in any more illegal activities. In August of 1997 Lee was arrested after being caught looking into the windows of a woman. Then, two years later to the month, he was arrested after being caught in a woman's residence uninvited, for being a Peeping Tom and stalking. His last activity in the 1990s was a December, 1999 suspended sentence that he received on a misdemeanor stalking charge.[18]

In January of 2000 Lee was accused of attempted first-degree murder after severely kicking and stomping his girlfriend Consandra Green at a bar after an argument over Lee's advances towards another woman. While trying to flee from the police following the incident he allegedly tried to run over the sheriff's deputy with a car. Lee was sentenced to two years for the incident. There are legitimate reasons for the public to question why Lee was let off the hook for this crime. Then, in September of 2001 Lee was arrested for battery against his wife but charges later dismissed. This was also the month that he murdered his first victim in Baton Rouge, Gina Green.[19]

Following the release of Lee's vast criminal history, people in Baton Rouge were shocked that he was never suspected in the local murders there, especially when the focus was changed to a man of color after a press conference in late March of 2003. Moreover, the task force was heavily criticized because Lee had been overlooked after having been brought to their attention by the Zachary Police Department in 2002. The Zachary Police suspected Lee in the murder of forty-one-year old Connie Warner in 1992 and the disappearance of twenty-year old Randi Mebruer in 1998. Despite the mistakes made in the case, the Task Force was congratulated by several public officials for their work in catching the killer.[20]

On August 5, 2004, Derrick Todd Lee's trial into the murder of Geralyn De Soto began in Port Allen, Louisiana. Ironically enough, DeSoto's death had not been one that was on a lot of people's minds during the spring of 2003, the tie between her death and the serial killer being made well after Lee's arrest. One of the first witnesses to be heard by the six men, six women jury and district judge Robin Free was one of Lee's last victims, Diane Alexander of Breaux Bridge, Louisiana. Her attack was discussed in the discussion group at the time it occurred, although the woman's name was not widely known at the time.[21] Alexander was one of the few that had apparently been attacked but not killed by Lee. Alexander pointed to him and said during her testimony, "while my eyes were closed, I did not forget your face." She had been beaten so severely during the July 2002 attack that her eyes were swollen shut. Alexander was one of several witnesses to testify against Lee that day.[22]

The following day Lee interrupted the testimony of the coroner who examined DeSoto's remains to "ask the judge to fire his court-appointed lawyer." According to press reports, Lee told the judge, "My life is on the line here" and that he wanted DeSoto's parents "to find out the truth about what happened to their daughter." Lee claimed that his lawyer lied to him and did not represent him properly. However, Lee and his lawyer were able to solve their problems and Tommy Thompson continued to represent him during the remainder of the trial.[23]

Another of the more riveting moments of the trial came when DeSoto's husband, Darren, testified to how he found his wife's body. According to press reports, Darren came home and found his wife lying on their bed in a "pool of blood." He was quoted in an article as saying, "I turned her head a little bit and at that moment I saw her throat was cut wide open." There's no doubt that his testimony made a lasting impression on the jury.[24] For months, Darren had been the focus of investigation amidst reports that he had physically abused his wife.[25]

Just four days later the jury deliberated. It took the jury only an hour and 40 minutes to come to a verdict. Eleven of the 12 jurors found Lee guilty of second-degree murder in the case of Geralyn DeSoto. Six days later, Judge Free sentenced Lee to life in Louisiana State Penitentiary at Angola," without the benefit of parole, probation or suspension of sentence."[26]

During sentencing, DeSoto's family confronted Lee about the murder of their daughter. Press coverage noted that DeSoto's father, John Barr, "locked eyes with Lee and told him, 'You don't know how bad I want to get a little closer to you.'" He was further quoted as saying "Thank God my daughter gave her soul to Christ before you took it. We know where your soul is going."[27]

In September 2004, Derrick Todd Lee faced his second murder trial, this time for the murder of Charlotte Murray Pace who had been beaten then stabbed to death with a screwdriver and a knife at her home in 2002. At the De Soto murder trial the prosecution decided not to go after the death sentence because they "couldn't prove the required 'aggravating circumstances,' such as a rape committed with a murder, to secure a death sentence," according to a press release. However, Lee's second trial for Pace's murder was different and of specific interest to the families of the murdered victims because for the first time he faced the death penalty by lethal injection as a possible outcome of the trial.[28]

Realizing this, the defense team, led by Mike Mitchell and Nelvil Hollingsworth made every effort to make sure Lee got a fair trial. Initially, they argued to have the trial moved to another location and have the pool of potential jurors tossed out because of concerns that the ceaseless media coverage of the murders and Lee's arrest would bias the jury. However, State District Judge Richard Anderson, who was presiding over the case, rejected the defense arguments believing that it would indeed be possible to find an unbiased jury. After some delays, the trial finally went ahead.[29]

The prosecution team, headed by John Sinquefield and Dana Cummings began their arguments by linking DNA samples taken from Lee with those found at the crime scene. Cummings suggested that DNA, which she referred to as "the silent witness" could actually "identify someone so particularly, so reliably, so exactly" that it was irrefutable evidence. In fact, police DNA expert Julia Naylor took the stand and stated that Lee's genetic profile was so rare that statistically there was a "one in 3.6 quadrillion (or 1,000 trillion) chance that the DNA would match any randomly selected person." In response to the genetic evidence, the defense questioned the methods used to collect DNA samples and the accuracy of the analysis conducted by an unaccredited lab, finding it inaccurate and unacceptable.[30]

The prosecution also tried to link Lee to the murders of Pam Kinamore and Carrie Yoder, whose murders bore marked similarities to Pace's. They presented DNA evidence taken from Lee that matched samples found at the crime scenes of all three victims. Moreover, the prosecution revealed that all victims exhibited similar bruising on their arms and hands, as well as neck injuries, which they likely received while trying to protect themselves during the struggle. All three women had been brutally raped before being killed. The defense retorted by questioning other items at the scene that were neither linked to Lee or the victims, suggesting that someone else was responsible for the crime.[31]

The defense did not present their own witnesses to support their arguments but instead relied on cross-examining the ones called by the prosecution. One such witness that took the stand was Diane Alexander who had survived an attack by Lee in 2002 and who had also testified at Lee's first trial. She told jurors her account of how Lee beat and attempted to rape her before being scared off by her son. Even though the defense questioned her memory of the event, Alexander stuck to her story stating that she had never taken her eyes off of Lee and that she clearly remembered the attack.[32]

Alexander's testimony coupled with the forensic evidence proved to have a significant impact on the jury. On October 12, 2004, after deliberating for just 80 minutes, jurors returned their verdict, finding Lee "guilty" of first degree-murder. Pace's mother Ann broke down crying after the verdict was read. She said that her daughter ... "somewhere must be real proud that it happened this way. There is evil in the world and he (Lee) is the personification of that." The next step that Lee had to face was the penalty hearing, in which the decision would be made concerning whether he would live or die.[33]

During the penalty hearing, jurors listened to conflicting statements made by mental health professionals concerning Lee's intelligence. According to the Supreme Court, a mentally retarded convict with an IQ below 70 must be exempted from the death penalty. Testimony by expert witnesses presented by the defense claimed that Lee was indeed retarded with an IQ between 62 and 65, making it difficult for him to understand the seriousness of his crimes.[34]

However, expert witnesses for the prosecution stated that Lee was not mentally retarded, basing their opinions on his decision-making ability and past work experience. Two men from a construction company where Lee worked as a pipe fitter also testified at the hearing. The men claimed that Lee excelled at his job and was able to read blueprints, which made it difficult to believe he had such a low IQ.[35]

Following the arguments the jury deliberated. After 93 minutes a verdict was returned. The jury rejected the defense team's contention that Lee was mentally retarded and sentenced him to death by lethal injection. Family and friends of the victims rejoiced, hugged and cried, most feeling that justice had finally been served.[36]

In December 2004, Lee was formally sentenced to death. His lawyers asked for a new trial, claiming that the jurors already were biased towards Lee before the Pace murder trial even commenced. Defense lawyers also filed documents for a new penalty hearing because Lee was mentally retarded and should not be put to death. Even though a judge has denied both requests, Lee's lawyers still plan to appeal.[37]

A press report stated that: "In addition to Pace and DeSoto, Lee has been indicted on a count of first-degree murder in the death of Trineisha Dene Colomb of Lafayette, and booked on first-degree murder counts in the deaths of Gina Wilson Green, Pam Kinamore, Carrie Lynn Yoder and Randi Mebruer, all of East Baton Rouge Parish." Yet, in January 2005, Colomb's family decided not to put Lee on trial, since he had already been convicted and sentenced to death. In the meantime, Lee spends what is left of his life in the Louisiana State Penitentiary at Angola.[38] It has been years, however, since Louisiana has executed a prisoner residing on Death Row.

ENDNOTES

1. *The Crime Library*, "Derrick Todd Lee," Chapter 5.

2. *Ibid.*

3. Godwin, *ibid.*

4. *The Crime Library*, Chapter 5.

5. *Ibid.*

6. *Ibid.*

7. *Ibid.*

8. *Ibid.*

9. This data is displayed on the main page of Dr. Godwin's discussion group.

10. Posted June 22, 2003.

11. Posted July 1, 2003.

12. Data for messages posted during 2004 appears on the main page of Dr. Godwin's discussion group.

13. *The Crime Library*, "Derrick Todd Lee," Chapter 5.

14. Maurice Godwin, *Tracker*, p. 139.

15. *The Crime Library*, Chapter 5.

16. *Ibid.*

17. *Ibid.*

18. *Ibid.*

19. *Ibid.*

20. *Ibid.*

21. Posted May 23, 2003.

22. *The Crime Library*, "The First of Many Trials," Chapter 17.

23. *Ibid.*

24. *Ibid.*

25. Stanley, *ibid.*

26. *The Crime Library*, Chapter 17.

27. *Ibid.*

28. *The Crime Library*, "Second Murder Trial," Chapter 13.

29. *Ibid.*

30. *Ibid.*

31. *Ibid.*

32. *Ibid.*

33. *The Crime Library*, "Deciding Lee's Fate," Chapter 14.

34. *Ibid.*

35. *Ibid.*

36. *Ibid.*

37. *Ibid.*

38. *Ibid.*

Chapter 7

Aftermath, Analysis and New Directions

In the hours and days following the capture of Derrick Todd Lee, activity on Dr. Godwin's discussion site had already begun to decline. In a manner thoroughly consistent with a postmodern, media driven society, public interest in the case took a nose dive during the months of June and July, when the emphasis was no longer on the identity of the killer, but on what the suspect was doing while in custody and how his case was progressing (or not) through Louisiana's criminal justice system. For many in Baton Rouge and in the discussion group, the case was over.

The group's hero, Maurice Godwin, had been publicly humiliated by Pat Englade in an interview following the capture of the serial killer. Mocking Godwin's model as being "20 miles off," Englade basked in the limelight of the Task Force's supposed accomplishment, though public anger would eventually come back to get him and oust him from office. For a short while at least, he was able to mock his critics and praise the work of the Task Force that he led.[1] It could be that some in the discussion group believed that Englade was right, and now they viewed all the faith they had previous put in Godwin to be misplaced.

The outspoken East Baton Rouge Coroner who would become the Louisiana's State Medical Examiner after Hurricane Katrina also slammed Godwin's method. Not mentioning it by name but dismissing it as a "cookie cutter approach," he was suspicious of slick new high tech ways to fight crime. He interpreted the triangular shaped area in the model as an absolute search area rather than an anchor point. An "old school" chum of Englade's, he favored slow, deliberate, old fashioned police work over newer technological approaches.[2] He clearly misunderstood Godwin's approach, as did the Task Force. Cataldie contended that Godwin's profile worked for the Gillis case but not for the Derrick Lee case. As Godwin pointed out, you do not mix data from two separate crimes in Predator.[3]

Something else that was bad for the morale of the internet social movement was the rapid demise of the related and more public movement, CASK. The leader of CASK was accused of using the organization's funds for personal gain, which only whipped up the opinion that the "compassion" that some group members supposedly held for the victims was all a "performance" whose purpose was to exploit the entire controversy for financial gain.[4] Press coverage of this story, beginning on June 3, was reposted to the discussion group:

> Members of CASK say several checks donated to the group were never deposited. Some members say this is all a big misunderstanding while others want answers even if it means turning in one of their own.

> You could always spot the members of CASK in a crowd by their bright green t-shirts. Anywhere there was a rally to support the search for the killer, they were sure to be there. They even traveled as far away as Lafayette urging women to stay alert.

> "We came together because we had a horrible monster facing this community and we wanted to help out," said CASK Vice President Nancy.

> A memo sent out to all members of CASK says the Division of Forgery and Financial Crimes has been contacted and an investigation is in the works.

> Nancy says, "We came together as a group and put forth great effort because we believed in what we were doing and we did want to help and this is an extreme misfortune and hopefully it can be recovered and we can find out the whereabouts of those checks."

> Nancy says they are uncertain how much money is missing, but there was an event in which members say they know some checks were written out to the group. However, when other members went to check the account, none of those checks had been deposited.

Nancy says all of the money was donated and they never asked for it. While companies donated many of the supplies they needed for flyers, some of the money was used to cover the cost of the t-shirts and other expenses.[5]

A CASK insider who participated in Dr. Godwin's group gave her account of what had happened inside CASK on June 3:

During the meeting Saturday, it was alleged that money from t-shirt sales should have been more. But it was also determined and agreed upon that so many had actually been donated away for various reasons, like to the victim's families and friends, that an accurate count could not be made and certainly didn't warrant an accusation of theft. Then there was mention of two fundraisers. The Secretary/Treasurer believes there are personal checks missing from (I think) one particular fundraiser. She's convinced there should have been more. So that's why the investigation was launched. I think I've presented both sides here. In all fairness, I have to say I have a great respect for and like every one of the ladies involved CASK. I feel in my heart there is so much more, but it would involve sheer speculation on my part so I'd rather not go there. It seems as if we have just traded one emotional roller coaster ride with D.T.L. for another. Hopefully all will be better soon.[6]

By June 4, the investigation had narrowed to one or two people:

Authorities are investigating the potential misuse of contributions to an organization founded during the Louisiana serial killings, a member of the organization says.

Chad Robinson, who called himself a founding member of Citizens Against Senseless Killings, said the allegations are against one or two people.

Robinson said he has been told that the East Baton Rouge Parish sheriff is investigating.

"Everything is allegations at this point," he said Tuesday. "We don't know if they're for real or not."

… CASK, a nonprofit organization, had been formed in reaction to the killings. It was originally called Citizens Against the Serial Killer, Robinson said.

"But we knew they'd catch the killer and then we'd move on," he said. "CASK is not going away."

Col. Mike Barnett, the sheriff's chief criminal deputy, said he could not confirm whether the organization was under investigation.[7]

Finally, the identity of the guilty party surfaced on June 24:

One of the founders of the nonprofit organization started in response to the south Louisiana serial killings is being investigated for pocketing more than $650 in donations, documents show.

Lisa Davis, 41, the former president of Citizens Against Senseless Killings, came under investigation last month, according to paperwork filed by the East Baton Rouge Parish Sheriff's Office.

In May, CASK officers questioned Davis about discrepancies in the group's financial records, according to documents supporting a subpoena filed in the investigation. "Ms. Davis could not adequately explain the discrepancies, and when deposits were later made by Davis there was still a shortfall," the document says. "Total losses to CASK from March 2003 to May 2003 exceed $650 in cash."

Sheriff's Office spokesman Lt. Darrell O'Neal said Monday the investigation is ongoing, but declined further comment.

Earlier this year, Davis said she is an emergency medical technician and mother of two. She did not return phone calls Monday. CASK was born on an Internet message board shortly after the slaying of 26-year-old Carrie Yoder, an LSU graduate student, had been linked to a serial killer.

Davis was among the founding members.

The group changed its name from Citizens Against the Serial Killer during the past month, about the time Derrick Todd Lee, 34, of St. Francisville was arrested in connection with the murders. Shortly after its founding, CASK began a series of fund-raisers, including a day-long tent sale in mid-April, with proceeds going to the organization.

Christina Blouin, who runs the shopping center on Jefferson Highway that hosted the event, said she severed ties with CASK shortly after the fund-raiser.

She said Davis wanted all the cash raised that day, but Blouin insisted on giving her a check a day later. Blouin ended up writing a check for $464 to CASK, she said. Blouin said she also spent $2,000 of her own money to advertise the event. "I've never done so much for someone and felt so unappreciated," she said. On June 5, sheriff's investigators got state District Court permission to obtain "any and all" documents from Davis' accounts at the Bank of Zachary, either in her name or in CASK's. "Monies were obtained through donations at events and by mail to a post office maintained by Davis," says the motion requesting the subpoena. The organization has printed T-shirts and created crosses featuring the names of more than 60 women whose deaths remain unsolved in south Louisiana.

Davis has declined to reveal her last name in interviews, instead going by her Internet pseudonym, Lady Medic, or Lisa Dee. [8]

Here is a final account in which clarifying information is revealed about the guilty party:

Police Arrest Former Head of CASK For Alleged Theft

The head of an organization formed at the height of serial killer fear has been arrested on theft charges. Baton Rouge Police arrested Lisa Davis, the former president of Citizens Against the Serial Killer, on charges she allegedly stole hundreds of dollars from money donated to the group.

No one disputes that Davis used $800 of her own money to get the group started, however, she is accused of failing to make the necessary deposits of $940. A warrant issued for Davis' arrest says aside from the money collected at rallies, people could also mail-in donations. The affidavit says the group maintains a post office box where donations are mailed but the treasurer and other board members were denied access to the box. The affidavit says Davis is the only one who had access to the money.

When authorities questioned Davis about the money, the Affidavit says the accused was unable to recall what she did with it and was also unable to provide an explanation of why the deposits were not made.

The affidavit says Davis eventually found the money in her son's car, but went on to say that was contrary to statements made by her son because according to the affidavit he told authorities she did not have access to his car.

Davis maintains, in the affidavit, that she did not use the funds to reimburse her initial $800 deposit and that there is no missing money. Meanwhile, CASK now stands for Citizens Against Senseless Killings. In a statement by the group, members say this has been a difficult time but their mission and belief is to always strive to do the right thing.[9]

This final report was intriguing in that it finally demonstrated how closely Dr. Godwin's group was stitched together with the above ground CASK. It appears in retrospect that Lisa Davis was undoubtedly the Leslie Davis that had participated so prolifically in the discussion group. Apparently she led a double life as she posted in large quantities to the *Court TV* site as Lady Medic. Davis is the one that had posted an estimated 400 messages to Godwin's site between March and May, 2003. A biographical sketch of Davis posted to a site not related to the serial killer revealed a former occupation of emergency medical technician, matching that of the woman convicted of stealing CASK's funds.[10] None of her original messages now appear in Godwin's message archive, and I suspect she was banned from the group immediately after her arrest. Charges were dropped against Davis in 2004. However, in the discussion group there was no discussion at all of the dropping of the charges; people had gone on to other things. Skeptics no doubt feasted on the fact that the movement to catch the serial killer was just one more example of corrupt politics as usual in Red Stick.

While this whirlwind of activity happened relatively soon after the capture of Lee, Godwin seem undeterred. Though modest, Godwin was trying hard not to gloat over some aspects of the case. Initially stung by the fact that the perpetrator's most recent home in the area had been St. Francisville, and that it was evidence in a Zachary case that provided the key link, Godwin still had faith in his approach. In fact it did point in the right direction, if only investigators would have taken him seriously. As he wrote on May 26: "Work office location and address (of Derrick Lee) on the sex offender registry is just outside my predicted area."[11] And again on May 29: "If the task force had used zip codes ending in 01 and 02 (which is in my predicted area) and swabbed only individuals who lived and worked in those areas with burglary records Lee would have been flushed out."[12] Finally, an important discovery on May 30: "According to Lee's records he listed his work address as 9700 Airline Hwy., which is the address of J.E. Merit Constructors. I found out today that the Merit office on Scenic closed down sometime ago. 9700 Airline Hwy. is just down the road 0.4 tenths of a mile from my exact predicted street Emmett Bourgeois, Ln."[13] It would appear, then, that Godwin was vindicated by the evidence. And later data that he presented in his book *Tracker* indicated that Lee had a steady girlfriend, Sheila O'Neal, who lived near the wedge-shaped predicted area. This place of residence was an anchor point for Lee as he planned and carried out several of the Baton Rouge murders.[14] It's entirely possible too, that the rapid departure of the people in his group was due to the fact that discussion group participants were relieved that Lee was captured but thoroughly fed up with the Task Force. They had criticized it all they could, and at some point enough is enough. If only the Task Force has listened to outside consultants such as Godwin, a few of the victims might be alive today.

Whether Godwin was viewed as a hero or goat, the fact is that members in his discussion group headed for the exits faster than the visitor's section at Death Valley, LSU's football stadium on game day. Following a high of 1,794 messages in May, 2003, the number had dwindled down to just 94 two months later and there were only 120 more messages posted during the rest of 2003. This residual discussion was mostly about Lee, his upcoming trial, his incarceration, and other cases to which he was being linked. Godwin was an active participant and continued to use the group as a mouthpiece to criticize the Task Force.[15]

We may never know the exact reasons why people drop out of such postmodern movements so quickly, although it is a common practice according to Pauline Rosenau and other experts. We will see what such experts have to say about that later. For now, we can observe that once such postmodern missions are over, the social movement dissolves and goes on to other interests. That was exactly what happened in California at the *Carl's Jr. Hamburgers* protest. A broad coalition of people opposed to the hamburger joint's policy of hiring whites only kept the pressure on until the restaurant began to hire minorities. When that began to happen, the movement was over.[16]

By the time Dr. Godwin's book *Tracker* came out, I was surprised to find the tone of the chapters on the Baton Rouge serial killer to be subdued, almost forlorn. With reflection, Godwin apparently viewed the whole case as an opportunity lost rather than a triumph of his high-tech methods over the slow and painful gumshoe approach. In an episode of academic honesty that was both refreshing and exceedingly rare, Dr. Godwin admitted in *Tracker* that his geographic model was only as good as the data that was known to the researcher and that was being input to the model, and that important information that is not taken account of by the model could still be out there and still be very important in solving the case. That was the case here where Godwin and just about everyone else failed to link the murders of Randi Mebruer and Connie Warner to Derrick Lee.[17] Godwin blamed the Task Force for not trying to share information with or to seek out information from, the other parishes nearby Baton Rouge. Even Englade's pal Louis Cataldie was brutally frank in his criticism of the Task Force, stating that sharing information with authorities from other jurisdictions is part of "Investigation 101" and there was no excuse for Englade keeping his information so close to the vest.[18]

A special feature of postmodern movements is that they are media driven. The media image is the most sought after commodity and it gives justification and legitimacy to the quest of the social movement, whatever it might be. Once this media show is over, the social movement dissolves. That was what happened in the Baton Rouge serial killer case.

That in turn got me to thinking about what the motives really were in this case for those who belonged to the discussion group. Did they want to be the one credited with breaking the case? Did they seek only the media spotlight? Maybe that's what they wanted all along. Leslie Davis used the controversy for her own gain. Maybe she thought that this would be her fifteen minutes of fame along with book and movie contracts, and an easier life. Even for Dr. Godwin, cracking the case would add to his growing legend as an expert and one who can use high tech means to solve any case, anywhere.

If this is true, then there is something called "media hunger" that surrounds the postmodern social movement. The media spotlight is sacrosanct. And it is also true that such movements are focused and perhaps even obsessed with a single event rather than with a more general cause. If, for instance, the discussion group was all about solving the general social problem of women being killed in Baton Rouge, then the movement would still be going and discussions in the group would still be brisk. It turned out that in the end, the person everyone wanted to be was an old-fashioned flat foot cop who investigated things the slow, low tech way. His name is Danny Mixon.

Mixon, the Attorney General's Office investigator who linked what was going on in Zachary to Derrick Todd Lee, was the unsung hero of the case. As he told the audience at one of Lee's pretrial hearings for the Pace murder, he had been tracking Lee for years. Mixon said he first began looking at Lee in 1999 when he was asked to assist the Zachary Police Department with investigations into the into the disappearance of Randi Mebruer in 1998 and the August 1992 slaying of Connie Warner, both of whom lived in Zachary which is about 24 miles from Baton Rouge. Zachary officers identified Lee as a suspect in the Mebruer case, Mixon said, so he kept track of where Lee worked and what vehicle he was driving. Mixon also said he kept up with the serial-killer investigation via media accounts. He said it was through his monitoring of Lee and the serial-killer investigation that he made the connection. "When I worked this all up, I though Derrick Todd Lee was the most viable suspect on the streets."[19] Mixon had pulled off the feat that everyone in Baton Rouge hoped to accomplish, including those in Dr. Godwin's discussion group: to match their proposed serial killer candidate with the DNA evidence.

Mixon had worked the Mebreur case for many years and to say he was involved with it is an understatement: it was more like an obsession. And for the longest of time he was completely convinced that the husband, Michael Mebreur was the killer. He covered Michael like a blanket. His coverage of the suspect was so intensive that, as he once told an interviewer, " … when Mebreur farted, I knew about it."[20]

What was the key to Mixon's success? He just did what every other old fashioned gumshoe would do, he followed up on a tip. This tip came from a semi-retired grocer named James Odom.

Odom, a retired grocer who lived in Jackson, Louisiana spent most of his days in 1998 tending to his cow and pasture land. One day while working on a job that required some help with heavy lifting, he hired on a local man who did odd jobs by the name of Leroy Shorts. Leroy and Odom began talking about the Mebruer case which was still fresh at the time, and Shorts said he had information about the case.[21]

Shorts lived next door to Lee's girlfriend of the moment, Consandra Green. As Lee was a frequent visitor there, Lee and Shorts became friends. One evening about midnight, Lee stormed into Shorts' house claiming that people were following him. He asked if Shorts would ride along with him to St. Francisville as Lee needed to take care of some business there. Shorts reluctantly agreed, and went along for the ride. Lee was nearly hysterical, was driving too fast, and appeared to be jumping at his shadow. The next day, when Shorts learned of Mebruer's disappearance on the news, he had little trouble connecting Lee to the event. Odom immediately reported Shorts' suspicions to the Zachary police, and found that Lee was already a suspect in the case.[22]

James Odom probably deserves as much credit as Mixon in bringing the case to closure. Odom was obsessed with the case, and was especially feeling that Lee was the killer of Mebruer and the Baton Rouge serial killer, especially after the March 21 news conference in which the Task Force noted that they were no longer looking for a white man, but someone of any race. Odom got his son Joel to contact an Attorney General's Office investigator and to express his concerns. A few days later, Mixon showed up at Odom's farm.[23]

Mixon thought the information was interesting, but was not jubilant at the tip. He knew from long experience that so called great leads often amount to nothing and that obscure ones can sometimes hit the jackpot. What intrigued him about the information was that it was new information, he had not seen one written report or heard anything about it through the rumor mill.[24]

Credit Mixon also with a measure of open mindedness that was truly remarkable. When he went to interview Odom, he spent a considerable amount of time trying to talk him out of the tip, as Mixon was already quite sure that his pet suspect, Michael Mebruer was the killer. Odom almost left the interview, but Mixon encouraged him to speak his mind. Mixon listened. Not long after that, Mixon began to put together the timeline of Lee that would ultimately lead to his arrest and conviction. Convinced now that Lee was the killer, he approached a judge for a court order to get a DNA swab from Lee. Court order in hand, he headed to St. Francisville along with colleagues on May 5, 2003, and the rest, as they say, is history.[25]

Mixon got no accolades at all from anyone, it seemed. At the press conference announcing the capture of Lee, Mixon was not invited, nor was the Zachary Police Department that he worked with to solve the case. Mixon's name was not mentioned at the press conference and it would be some time before reporters tracked him down and got his story.

There was little celebration of Mixon in the discussion group and it appeared that this once dynamic social movement, as well as most of the citizens of Baton Rouge, was seeking respite from the emotionally grueling hunt for the serial killer. Louis Cataldie said it was really a matter of fatigue: people were just plain tired of it.[26]

In a manner that was thoroughly postmodern, the public's attention after Lee's arrest shifted quickly to other things, and it soon forgot the serial killer case as the LSU football team made its run at a collegiate national championship. The most drastic fall off in the messages posted to Dr. Godwin's group was during July, as the first of the preseason hype touting LSU's football team hit the press. Following an early season loss to Florida, LSU faced a "win or else" situation in all of their games from that time forward, and as they continued to win, the stakes got higher each week. They found themselves in the running for the SEC West Championship, then the SEC Championship, and then the National Championship. By defeating Oklahoma in the Sugar Bowl, 21-14, LSU claimed a share of the Division I national championship of college football for 2003, and its reputation as one of the most dangerous campuses in the world for female students appeared to be all but forgotten. Instead, the legend of Death Valley was growing.

Also buried under the football hype was the shooting at a Southern University football game on October 8, 2005 that injured three fans attending the game at A.W. Mumford Stadium in Baton Rouge.[27] This was part of a national acceleration of campus violence and something that should have been alarming at the street level but was not interesting at all to the citizens of Baton Rouge: perhaps indeed they were feeling some "serial killer fatigue" as Cataldie had suggested, following the long hunt for Derrick Lee.[28]

As a citizen and a social activist, I was personally appalled at how quickly public interest waned with respect to solving the remaining unsolved murders in Baton Rouge. I have to admit on a personal level that people do move on to other things; for example, I was preparing a book proposal for a small university press beginning in the fall of 2003, so my own interest in the case diminished to a degree. But with nearly 70 women still missing, more work needed to be done. It appears in retrospect that some in the discussion group just wanted to become famous for fingering the serial killer and for seeing that their own pet theory in the case was the one that mattered. They wanted to do what Danny Mixon had done, and to follow up the feat with book and movie contracts. As early as July, 2003, almost all of the sense of injustice that had fueled the movement in the first place had vanished. The fact that many of the missing were poor Black women from the poorer parts of Baton Rouge, and some were suspected prostitutes should not have deterred people in the search for their killer. Are these women somehow less important than the lives of the women killed by Derrick Todd Lee? I was concerned by the blatant racism that this suggested, and I had to rationalize this anomaly by contemplating for a moment that not that long ago, the state legislature in Louisiana had an office for a young man named David Duke, who was viewed by most people nationally as a political extremist and racist.[29] Then, I remembered the images of the scene at the Louisiana Superdome and the New Orleans Convention Center after Hurricane Katrina put things in perspective; the sea of people waiting for evacuation buses were poor and Black, and this is a state that has demonstrated through its actions (or lack thereof) and not its words that it really does not care about people who are poor and Black.[30]

As a sociologist, my professional experience working on this case proved more satisfying as I was able to validate some fundamental ideas from social theory and how those theories help to explain how social movements develop, mature, and pass away. The Baton Rouge case appeared to fit numerous ideas about social movement development that have been written about over the years. For instance, an initial stage in social movements is the beginning of feelings of injustice about a matter that get voiced amidst feelings of tension or social strain.[31] Certainly there was strain and tension as the murders mounted and the possibility was increasing that they were the work of one person. Then, as a second step, ideas circulate among a group of people that provides the basis for further action. In the Baton Rouge case, there was a general belief that not enough was being done by the Task Force to find the killer. Third, certain events precipitate action, and then leaders step forward to activate the movement. In Baton Rouge, Carrie Yoder's death was the precipitant, and Dr. Godwin's strong leadership became the force that initiated and shaped a social movement on the Internet.[32] This of course was not the only source of activism as CASK and the victims' families mobilized offline to put pressure on the Task Force.

The literature on social movements also suggests that movements can be classified according to their purposes. Some are reformative, seeking to reform some aspect of society. Others are transformative or revolutionary. Revolutions such as those in the American colonies, France, Russia and Cuba are examples of the latter.[33] From the preceding it should be fairly obvious that the Internet movement and CASK based in Baton Rouge are more reflective of reforming some aspect of society rather than transforming it. Here the focus is clearly on the reformative action of eliminating the serial killer threat, and there is the closely connected and larger societal issue of making Baton Rouge safer for women. This is an issue that, if Baton Rouge is successful, the good results of that effort can be copied elsewhere, and the reforms of Baton Rouge can be shared with other cities.

At the same time, the argument could be made that Maurice Godwin's movement and all the others in Baton Rouge did not fit neatly into this traditional way of classifying social movements. For example, while the purpose of the Internet movement was to eliminate serial killer behavior among individuals, whoever might be participating in that behavior, it was clear as time wore on that the movement hinged on catching one person and one person only, Derrick Todd Lee, and eliminating his personal killing behavior. Thus, in retrospect we could observe that the goal was not to change the behavior of *all* the individuals engaged in serial killing in the Baton Rouge area. That this was the case was obvious because, once Lee was caught, the movement seemed to disappear into thin air. Nor can we say that the Internet movement was trying to reform society as a whole in a meaningful way by eliminating all of its serial killers in south Louisiana or anywhere else. If that was the case, the movement would have survived online, as well as in CASK, well past the capture of Derrick Todd Lee and probably would have been around at least until the second Baton Rouge suspect has been apprehended in 2004. We know, however, that this was not the case. And with many more cases unsolved at the end of 2006, there is much, much more work to be done in Baton Rouge, yet, the Internet social movement (and CASK) is completely inactive at this time. Not a single message has been posted since December, 2006. If its purpose was to truly reform society, more people would be interested and participating in the group at the current time.

Why is it that people leave social movements, particularly now, in postmodern times where they take their leave suddenly and without much notice? For that, some background about postmodernism is needed.

By the 1980s scholars believed that many social movements displayed characteristics different from those of earlier times, especially the 1960s style activist movements such as the anti-Vietnam War movement. The new social movements rejected theories or grand explanations, focused on cultural strategies that combined personal and collective actions, and displayed a more decentralized form of organization.[34] This transition appeared to set the stage for postmodernism.

In the 1990s, postmodern theories swept through the landscape of sociology, making an impact upon the way that sociologists viewed the world.[35] Today, postmodern social theory takes its place alongside structural functionalism, conflict theory, symbolic interaction, and feminism as a major explanation for why people behave as they do. In essence, postmodernism is counterintuitive and basically opposed to the other theories mentioned. It questions just about every social thought that emanated from modernist thinkers following the Enlightenment. A full chapter could be written about this brand of theory, but its major differences from "modern" theories or those of the post Enlightenment are briefly summarized below.

Consider a few of the more fundamental assumptions of modern science: 1) that there is some kind of discoverable order to the universe, and 2) that knowledge of this order is something desirable or useful. These assumptions fueled all kinds of science since the Enlightenment, from engineering and biology to the social sciences of psychology and sociology. Basically, these assumptions embody why science is pursued in the first place, from basic to advanced research. Postmodernism, as a counterintuitive tool of critiquing modernity, sharply questions these assumptions. Postmodernists would argue that instead of their being order in the universe, there is only a chaos that is unknowable. Instead of there being a knowledge that is desirable, there is no knowledge whatsoever.

As a counterweight of sorts that is balanced against this pessimism, there is a more positive variant of postmodernism that suggests there is some benefit to be gained from engaging in tactics that are part modern or even semi-modern. This affirmative postmodernism might put forth the argument that there is some order in the universe and that it is partly knowable. Concerning knowledge, there can be some measure of it. These more optimistic postmodernists emphasize local knowledge as being important, and eschew grand explanatory schemes or large theories as a source of knowledge, or even large accumulations of knowledge in pursuit of a universal or overarching kind of knowledge.

The movements in Baton Rouge against the serial killer appear to tap directly into this vein of affirmative postmodernism, and that is why I suggest that Maurice Godwin's Internet movement may someday be held up as a "classic" example of this kind of movement. It was local in origin and had to do with the serial killings and the safety of women in Baton Rouge. Dr. Godwin from the beginning insisted that the movement be local. He limited membership in the group, with a few exceptions, to people in Baton Rouge or south Louisiana, as this was the community of people most directly in the path of the terrifying criminal stalking their neighborhoods. Second, consider the kind of knowledge that was being pursued. It was not so much a discourse on serial killers in general but on this one case in particular, and how some innovative new ideas that appeared counterintuitive to traditional criminology and police work might help to crack the case wide open. The purpose of Dr. Godwin's new geographic model was not so much to promote universal knowledge as to promote local knowledge of one specific case, and as such fits the mode of affirmative postmodern inquiry.[36] He spent a good deal of time teaching the group his model of geographic mapping that ultimately would work quite well in the Derrick Todd Lee case. He admonished people whose wild speculations strayed too far from the known facts that were the raw data for his geographic mapping calculations. Yet, he allowed informed speculations within the realm of what was already known about the case.

Pauline Rosenau notes in her book on postmodernism that postmodern social movements tend to be organized along ad hoc issues, and that they are often temporary, disappearing after an issue has been "solved" to a community's satisfaction. This appears to fit perfectly what happened in Baton Rouge. The serial killer case developed as an ad hoc issue: it was not even known for sure that the killings were linked to one perpetrator until the last half of 2002 with the death of Pam Kinamore, and from there the issue took off instantly as a critical issue to be solved locally. And, we know that it was basically a temporary movement. Upon the capture of Derrick Lee, the movement essentially collapsed.

Rosenau further suggested that there may be "crossover participation" in the ad hoc social movement. That is, people whose concerns are similar to, but not the same as those in the ad hoc movement join forces. This means that the movement at times may represent an unusual pastiche that looks from time to time like strange bedfellows. In the example that Rosenau gives from the 1990s that was certainly the case. It was the case of a *Carl's Jr. Hamburgers* protest in California. The initial issue had to do with the hiring of minorities. The hamburger outlet, a competitor of McDonald's and Burger King, appeared to be hiring only white people in one California town. Minorities got involved in the movement early on, but as time wore on, others joined in the fray: animal rights activists who criticized the outlet's killing of animals to produce beef; handicapped activists said that the outlet was not handicap accessible, and these in turn brought their own gaggle or entourage of sympathizers. It seemed that everyone that had a "beef" with the restaurant was protesting. It was an unusual coalition to say the least, and that is what Rosenau meant by crossover participation.

In Baton Rouge something similar appeared to be taking place, although our ability to draw conclusions is at times limited by the very structure of the Internet discussion groups. For example, in the Internet social movement many people who posted messages hid behind aliases or "handles" and did not reveal their true identity. Some revealed their occupations but others didn't. Nonetheless, it could be deduced from direct observation that some of the interested persons were people interested in women's issues in general, and were drawn into the fray on that basis. People who were interested in self-defense training were drawn in, as they saw their training as something important that would or could be used to protect themselves. And politically, it drew women of all political stripes and persuasions who feared for their own safety and that of their constituents. CASK drew a diverse group as well, with both Democratic and Republican women showing an interest in the fledgling social movement.

Beyond that, the appeal was quite general and attracted a potpourri of interested persons, each apparently interested for their own reasons. Judging from the memos or messages posted to the Internet, the people interested in the case covered a wide range of humanity from professors and other professionals to feminists to people interested in women's interests in general, to true crime addicts who absorb themselves in the case of the moment whatever that might be: Laci Peterson case, the Baton Rouge case, the Natalie Holloway case, or whatever case happens to be in the news at that moment. Given the success of *Court TV*, this media-driven constituency may have been one of the largest. And then, there were people seeking publicity or economic gain from the case, hoping that their nomination for serial killer turned out to be the correct one, or that their theory proved to be the right and true once all the data had come in. This is the "media hunger" that I've been talking about. Given the way that the movement virtually collapsed after May, 2003, one suspects that there were a good number of these kinds of people in the Internet movement.

The social organization of cyberspace allowed the movement to stake its ground quickly and to hit the ground running. The *Yahoo!* discussion group functioned as a large bulletin board which members could access at their leisure and post comments to at any time that is convenient for them. Comments had to be directed toward the subject matter and to deal with the facts known at the time. Dr. Godwin, as moderator, had the ability to ban individuals who were there to "spam" the group or to promote products or to promote themselves, and he did so on more than one occasion. This limitation of participation was an advantage that the *Yahoo!* groups had over earlier USENET discussion groups, which were open to all who could afford to subscribe and which tolerated most all postings in good taste on a "free speech" basis. It was difficult to ban people from USENET because they had paid for the service. The *Yahoo!* groups were free and one only needed to have access to the Internet and to provide two working email addresses along with evidence of an interest in the subject matter at hand. Then, importantly, the participants needed to adhere to the conduct norms of the discussion group.

Another way to reflect upon the Baton Rouge experience is to consider that the entire serial killer controversy in Baton Rouge took place within a postmodern media culture where the cultural meanings and understandings of the event are tied closely to the media images about the event that are being transmitted by the media and consumed by the public. As the influence of the media continued to grow, there was a corresponding difficulty to distinguish between that which was social reality as presented by the mass media, and that which is social reality as discoverable by other kinds of sense data. Some scholars believe that the media in general does its part to blur whenever possible the distinction between what the media reports and "social reality."[37] Alternative views of the news may not be allowed or presented, and with the public uncritically following the media's lead, the postmodern world assigns primacy to media coverage, so it's almost as if what is real is televised and if something is not televised, it is not real and it did not happen. In postmodern media culture, lack of press interest about a subject often translates into no public interest whatsoever in that subject.

Students of symbolic interaction (a prominent sociological theory) tell us that the cultural and media significance of dying has escalated in the postmodern era. That significance rests on the symbolic context in which representations of dying are embedded, and it became clear as time went on that symbolic context was as much entertainment as it was news. Scholars of the media noted as the 1980s approached that it was more difficult than ever to make a distinction between news and entertainment.[38] The death of a famous individual became not only news but a "story" to be told in an entertaining way. In the last quarter of the 20th century, television had become a major item of leisure time, and as such the postmodern society would be known for its intertwining of the media and people's daily lives and activities.[39] The women killed by Derrick Todd Lee had become, in death, public celebrities, and their stories were pursued not only for their news but also their entertainment value.

Though interest in the case vanished in a way consistent with postmodern movements, there was some residual interest in the case when a second serial killer was apprehended in 2004, and evidence in that case cleared a few more of the missing person cases. Sean Vincent Gillis, 41 years old and living at 545 Burgin St., was booked into Parish Prison on April 29, 2004 in the deaths of three women with high-risk lifestyles, according to Sheriff's Office records. Gillis, who is white, was booked in the deaths of Katherine Hall, 29, Johnnie Mae Williams, 45, and 43-year-old Donna Bennett Johnston. All three women had been arrested for prostitution, drugs or both. Records from the East Baton Rouge Parish Clerk of Court's Office show Gillis has been arrested once in the past, for criminal trespass in 1980.[40]

Given the large number of women still missing, even after the list of missing shortened a bit after the Gillis case, we are probably not at the end of the serial killer case in Baton Rouge. Dr. Godwin continued to show concern by continuing to moderate his group on the Internet despite little activity, perhaps sensing that he might have to come back to solve yet another case sometime in the future. The Task Force, for its part, ended the heavy lifting part of its work with the capture of Derrick Lee. One of its last communiqués to the public is a photo of Derrick Lee with the words "captured" written on it.[41]

By the time of the second killer's arrest, Pat Englade had retired as chief of Police in Baton Rouge. His resignation was seen as an effort to help his friend Bobby Simpson get reelected as mayor. His retirement did not help Simpson as he went down to defeat.

The thought of Englade writing his own book about the serial killer case sparked a mini-controversy of its own, one duly noted by the faithful remnant remaining in Godwin's discussion group. An article in the paper screamed, "Englade's Book Idea Not Sitting Well With Families; Serial Killer Task Force Made Serious Errors, Victim's Brother Says." The following is the press coverage of the controversy that was posted to the discussion group.

The controversy erupted after Englade began touring the country lecturing law enforcement agencies about the serial killer investigation. It seems that somewhere along the way, Englade had a change of heart about books on the investigation. Before a suspect was behind bars, Englade went before a group of concerned and angry citizens and explained to them why he didn't want any outside experts helping with the investigation. "I'm not looking to sell some books or movie rights or anything else," Englade told the group on March 26. "I can't trust that someone outside (an outside expert) does not have that interest in mind."[42]

At some point he changed his mind. "It's not a sensational book," he said, defending the idea. "It's not a Patricia Cornwell book." Englade said his book would help law enforcement agencies solve serial killer cases. "Unless it's a book on what they did wrong and all their oversights, I'd say it's an audacious and pompous notion," said Ed Piglia, Pam Kinamore's brother.[43] The discussion group agreed, being already notified of Mixon's quiet, unpublicized work that solved the case.

The public, of course, was learning the same thing: that the Louisiana serial killer case was cracked, not by someone on the Task Force, but by the detective from the Attorney General's Office, Danny Mixon. Then, about the time this controversy over Englade's book was erupting, it was learned that Task Force detectives had been given Lee's name early on in the investigation, but allegedly didn't consider him a suspect because they thought the man they were after was white. "Who knows how many women's lives could have been spared if they'd picked up that lead and picked up the suspect they should have," Piglia said.[44]

Englade said his speeches and his book are not about taking credit for solving the case. "Other law enforcement agencies don't care who caught Derrick Todd Lee," Englade said. "They want to know how it was organized and the methods you use, that's all they care about. It has nothing to do with credit."[45] Ironically enough, the Task Force should have gotten little or no credit as it was the Attorney General's Office, working with local police in Zachary that ultimately cracked the case.

Victims' family members hope that if Englade does write a book, he will donate profits to a charity or to organizations that help victims of crime. There is no word on whether Englade plans to do so.[46]

In response, a bit of the old moral outrage flared up once again in the discussion group, a post gleam of what once thrived there. One writer mocked the idea of Englade writing a book:

Although a serial killer investigation was conducted and they went through the process of that, I don't think the Task Force is qualified enough to be lecturing...unless to inform what NOT to do. I think it's nice of them to mention that they didn't actually catch the serial killer suspect. They should also mention that they had nothing to do with it.

They spent three hours a day preparing for the media. You know, I suspected the media might be the serial killer, too.

I want to know: who else finds it hypocritical of Englade to write a book? His big reason for avoiding outside help was because he didn't want them to exploit the family and victims.

Will the profits from this book go towards helping law enforcement and crime prevention?[47]

The thrill was gone, however, and the posting above stimulated little if any discussion.

What is happening now, in 2007? Are women safer today in Baton Rouge than they were in the past?

At a sexual assault prevention conference in Baton Rouge in 2004, the conference theme was "Where is the Outrage?" which is exactly what the remnant of Dr. Godwin's group was thinking. The meeting was all about highlighting the issue of women's safety and the need for keeping vigilant and alert. Sponsored by The Louisiana Foundation Against Sexual Assault, the conference was three days of plenary sessions, exhibits, and networking opportunities. A committee of representatives from the agencies co-sponsoring the conference, each of which deal with sexual assault issues in some capacity, designed a program that was hoped to be valuable for law enforcement officers, prosecutors, judges, nurses and physicians, emergency medical personnel, crime lab staff, child and adult protection staff, advocates, counselors, therapists, prevention educators, probation and parole officers, correction officers, and sex offender treatment providers, as well as other professionals. At this more academic level, there was an interest in keeping some of the moral outrage alive that had fueled the various victims groups, CASK, Dr. Godwin's Internet group, and other interested parties. This conference gave some hope that the practitioners who work with women every day might be part of an effort to help women stay on the watch and to stay alert. The spirit of the conference was that women could learn from events like the serial killer case and apply such lessons to daily life.[48]

Having said that, it is ironic to contemplate or even to imagine, with Lee now behind bars, that women might be at higher risk than ever before to assault by a sexual predator simply because of what happened in the wake of hurricanes Katrina and Rita which hit south Louisiana in August and September, 2005. With major portions of New Orleans and lower coastal areas of south Louisiana in ruins, this gave some practicing sexual predators an opportunity to disperse, to relocate, and to begin anew somewhere else far away from their homes and far away from the gaze of the public officials in charge of monitoring them. This included predators from Louisiana and from other states wanting to find a place to lay low and hide. Baton Rouge could now be one of several hiding places for such men. Meanwhile, the distractions of the hurricane relief effort, unfortunately, put women in new social patterns in which old familiar safeguards and practices may not be heeded or are forgotten. The population of Baton Rouge swelled with evacuees from New Orleans and south Mississippi and with relief workers coming in to help rebuild the most damaged areas. Some of these new and seemingly friendly "relief workers" could also be sexual predators in disguise. In all the confusion of these new social patterns, women could be more vulnerable than ever before to an attack by a sexual predator.

Derrick Lee, ironically enough, may have been given a reprieve of sorts by all the bad weather. The hurricanes may literally be extending his life. The Louisiana Supreme Court, which could be Lee's court of last resort, was closed except for emergency business in the fall of 2005, and in early 2006 was just getting back to what might be called a normal schedule. But there is a huge backlog of cases to consider now, including Lee's petitions. Lee could be getting some extra months of life out of this. Consider also that the delay gives his attorneys more time to work his case, including dealing with the issue of Lee's mental competencies. His lawyers may be able to find an expert that will assess Lee as mentally retarded and therefore argue that he is exempt from the death penalty under Louisiana law.

Danny Mixon is now retired. But consistent with his modest nature, he gives very few interviews about the serial killer case.

James Odom is still a retired grocer who deserves much credit for Derrick Todd Lee being behind bars, and still lives in Jackson, Louisiana.

The families of the serial killer's victims continue to be active in the movement for victim's rights.

Diane Alexander, one of the few to encounter Derrick Lee and live to tell about it, was rebuffed in her effort to collect the Crime Stoppers reward from information leading to Derrick Lee's capture and conviction. Despite lending critical testimony in Lee's first trial, she was denied her request for the Crime Stoppers funds.

CASK, renamed Citizens Against Senseless Killings after Lee's capture, had its filing as a corporation revoked by the Louisiana Secretary of State. Such revocations occur after three years of no activity.

Yvonne Welch continues to represent District 67, a Baton Rouge district, in the Louisiana House of Representatives.

Robert Keppel's criticisms of the Task Force's work back in 2003 were right on target. Just as he had suggested, the Task Force did have Lee's name early in the investigation, as early as April of 2002. In fact, a St. Francisville woman stalked by Lee called his name in to the Task Force. Releasing the DNA match between several of the victims did indeed cause Derrick Lee to alter his tactics, including the ditching of the potentially incriminating clothing. And the release of the psychological profile did add to the information overload and to the rampant speculation about who the killer could be. It seemed that everyone in south Louisiana had called in their village sociopath to the Task Force.

Dr. Maurice Godwin's book, *Tracker*, came out in the fall of 2005. There are two chapters about the Baton Rouge case. The book is a compendium of several cases he has worked, and the impression that one gets from the book is that the author is a very busy professional who excels at multi-tasking. It is clear now that he works several cases at once, and in late 2005 he was working on the Natalie Holloway case in Aruba. In addition, he becomes interested in new cases all the time and continues to employ his system, Predator, as an analytic tool in these new cases. One of his last posts to the group in February, 2006 was about an emerging case, the South Louisiana Highway Killer.

According to press reports that were reposted to the discussion group, sixteen murders have been documented along a strip of south Louisiana highway and a pattern has emerged. In what appeared to be the latest serial killer case, officials believe that the killer is targeting gay and bisexual men. The killings have been going on since 1997 and the most recent connected murder victim was found on April 27, 2005. Investigators have pictures of six who were found in the Houma area: 22 year old Leon Lirette was found in Houma; 23 year old Kurt Cunningham was found in Lafourche Parish hear Highway 307; 18 year old Datrell Woods was found in Houma; 20 year old Michael Barnett was also found in Houma; 31 year old August Watkins was found along Highway 90 in Lafourche Parish; and 26 year old Anoka Jones was from Houma but was found in Saint Charles Parish.

Most of the bodies have been found along the Highway 90 corridor going south toward New Orleans. Many of the victims have been found without shoes and had either been strangled or suffocated. The victims range in age from sixteen to forty-five years old, and the average age is twenty-five. Investigators think some of the victims were murdered in other parishes and dumped. The Attorney General's Office and the law enforcement agencies who are part of this task force aren't giving out much information, such as a description of the person they're looking for. They say they don't want to damage the investigation by releasing too much information. Despite this new case, there were no follow up postings at all to the discussion group. Even when the Highway Killer was apprehended and charged late in 2006, the arrest did little to arouse interest in the group.

Life goes on. Dr. Godwin still heads the discussion group that is highlighted in this book. I sincerely hope that his return to Baton Rouge is *not* in the offing, because such a trip would be to discuss new details of yet another emerging case. That can't be ruled out, considering the large cases there that are still unsolved, by my count almost 70. Certainly there are enough victims out there to entertain the idea that yet another serial killer may be out there preying on women in Baton Rouge.

ENDNOTES

1. Maurice Godwin, *Tracker*, p. 151.

2. Cataldie, *ibid*.

3. Posted May 4, 2004.

4. See Erving Goffman, *The Presentation of Self in Everyday Life*. Garden City: Double-day, 1959.

5. Posted June 3, 2003.

6. *Ibid*.

7. Posted June 4, 2003.

8. Posted June 24, 2003.

9. Posted July 3, 2003.

10. Internet search completed September 15, 2006.

11. Posted May 26, 2003.

12. Posted May 29, 2003.

13. Posted May 30, 2003.

14. Godwin, *Tracker*, p. 151.

15. Message traffic count was retrieved from the front page of the discussion group.

16. Pauline Rosenau, *Postmodernism and the Social Sciences*. Princeton: Princeton University Press, 1992.

17. Godwin, *ibid*.

18. Cataldie, *ibid*.

19. Posted on January 15, 2004.

20. Stanley, *ibid*.

21. *Ibid*.

22. *Ibid.*

23. *Ibid.*

24. *Ibid.*

25. *Ibid.*

26. *Ibid.*

27. James Turner, "Shooting Prompts Additional Safety," *The Southern Digest*, October 18, 2005.

28. At least 15 college shootings were recorded during 2005. See Stan Weeber, *Violence in Academe*, forthcoming; during 2006, there were shootings at Duquesne University and at a Canadian college.

29. John George and Laird Wilcox, *American Extremists*. Amherst, NY: Prometheus Books, 1996.

30. "Hurricane Katrina: Crisis in New Orleans." Center for Media and Democracy, accessed September 30, 2006.

31. Neil Smelser, *Theory of Collective Behavior*. New York: Free Press of Glencoe, 1963.

32. *Ibid.*

33. *Ibid.*

34. Bert Klandermans, "New Social Movements and Resource Mobilization: The European and American Approach." *International Journal of Mass Emergencies and Disasters*, 1986, 4, 2, August, 13-37.

35. Rosenau, *ibid.*

36. *Ibid.*

37. Dominic Strinati, *An Introduction to the Study of Popular Culture*. London: Routledge, 2000.

38. George Gerbner, "Death in Prime Time: Notes on the Symbolic Function of Dying in the Mass Media." *Annals*, 1980, 447, 64-70.

39. Strinati, *ibid*; Michael Moore and Linda Moore, "Fall from Grace: Implication of the O.J. Simpson Trial for Postmodern Criminal Justice." *Sociological Spectrum*, 1997, 17, 305-322.

40. Roy Pitchford, "Gillis Pleads Not Guilty." *Baton Rouge Advocate*, July 10, 2005.

41. See http://brgov.com/TaskForce

42. *WDSU.com*, "Englade's Book Idea Not Sitting Well With Families," November 13, 2003.

43. *Ibid.*

44. *Ibid.*

45. *Ibid.*

46. *Ibid.*

47. Posted November 6, 2003.

48. Second Annual Louisiana Sexual Assault Conference, "Where is the Outrage?" sponsored by the Louisiana Foundation Against Sexual Assault, December 8-10, 2004, Baton Rouge, Louisiana.

Bibliography

Adams, Jacqueline. 2005. "When Art Loses its Sting: The Evolution of Protest Art in Authoritarian Contexts," *Sociological Perspectives*, 48, 4, Winter: 531-558.

Baden, Michael. 1989. *Unnatural Death*. New York: Random House

Baton Rouge Advocate, 2003a. "DNA Evidence Links Murder of Carrie Lynn Yoder to the Serial Killer," March 18: 1.

———. 2003b. "Yoder's Body Recovered." March 14: 1.

BREC, The Recreation and Park Commission for the Parish of East Baton Rouge 2007. Available online at http://www.brec.org (accessed February 15, 2007).

Brinkley, Douglas. 2000. *Rosa Parks*. New York: Viking.

Burns, Kari Sable, 2005. "The Politics of Murder: Will Baton Rouge Clean House? Available online at: http://www.karisable.com/skazbr3.htm (accessed on September 3, 2005).

Cataldie, Louis. 2006. *Coroner's Journal*. New York: G.P. Putnam's Sons.

CBS Evening News. 2002. "A City Gripped by Fear," August 7.

CBS News. 2003. "A Serial Killer in Police Garb?" April 8.

Center for Media and Democracy. 2006. "Hurricane Katrina: Crisis in New Orleans." Available online at: http://www.prwatch.org/ (accessed September 30).

City Confidential. 2003. "Baton Rouge: Scandal on the Bayou," Episode 53, Season 5, aired August 2.

CNN, 2003. "'Major Development' in Louisiana Serial Killer Case," January 23.

Crime Library, 2005a. "Deciding Lee's Fate," available online at: http://www. crimelibary.com (accessed June 15).

———. 2005b. "Derrick Todd Lee," accessed September 3.

———. 2005c. "Hunting Evil," accessed September 3.

———. 2005d. "Second Murder Trial," accessed September 3.

———. 2005e. "The First of Many Trials," accessed June 15.

———. 2005f. "The Mystery of the Baton Rouge Serial Killer," accessed June 15.

Department of Biology, Louisiana State University. 2003. "In Carrie's Memory," available online at: http://www.lsu.edu/findcarrie/ (accessed June 1).

Dobie, Ann Brewster. 2006. *Wide Awake in the Pelican State*. Baton Rouge: Louisiana State University Press.

Finch, Susan. 2003. "Baton Rouge Man Sues for his DNA." *New Orleans Times Picayune*, June 3.

Flarity, Rachel. 2004. "Students Await Holden's Changes." *The Daily Reveille*. Louisiana State University, November 23.

Fund, John. 2005. "A Swamp of Corruption: In Katrina's Wake, Louisiana's Political Culture Needs a Cleanup Too," *Jewish World Review*, September 25.

Gaudet, Marcia and James C. McDonald (Eds.) 2003. *Mardi Gras, Gumbo, and Zydeco*. Jackson: University Press of Mississippi.

George, John and Laird Wilcox. 1996. *American Extremists*. Amherst, NY: Prometheus Books.

Gerbner, George. 1980. "Death in Prime Time: Notes on the Symbolic Function of Dying in the Mass Media." *Annals*, 447, 64-70.

Greater Baton Rouge Business Report. 2005. "True Crime," September 15.

Godwin, Maurice. 2006. Professional web page. Available online at: www. invest tigativepsych.com (accessed September 1).

———. 2005. *Tracker: Hunting Down Serial Killers*. New York: Thunder's Mouth Press.

Goffman, Erving. 1959. *The Presentation of Self in Everyday Life*. Garden City, NY: Doubleday.

Gunn, Robert. 2005. "Louisiana Supreme Court Closure," September 29.

Gyan, Joe. 2005. "Lee's Supreme Court Appeal Gets Number, Brief Deadlines." *Baton Rouge Advocate*, August 23.

Hallcox, Jarrett. 2006. *Bodies We've Buried*. New York: Berkley Books.

Haygood, Wil. 2006. "After Katrina, Baton Rouge Weathers a Storm of Its Own." *Washington Post*, August 25.

Henslin, James. 2005. *Essentials of Sociology*. Boston, MA: Allyn and Bacon.

Jackson, Paul and Jos van der Wielen. 2002. *Teleworking International Perspectives: From Telecommuting to the Virtual Organization*. New York: Routledge.

Johnson, Allen. 2003. "To Catch a Killer." bestofneworleans.com, February 4.

KATC, 2005. "Record of Derrick Todd Lee Trial Given to Supreme Court," Available online at http://www.katc.com, accessed September 3.

Klandermans, Bert. 1986. "New Social Movements and Resource Mobilization: The European and American Approach." *International Journal of Mass Emergencies and Disasters*, 4, 2, August: 13-37.

Kretzer, Karl. 2005. *Danced to Death: The Desperate Hunt for a Cross- Country Serial Killer*. Baltimore: PublishAmerica.

Masamichi, Inoue. 2005. "The Female Inheritance Movement in Hong Kong," *Current Anthropology*, 46, 3, June: 403.

Meyers, Rose. 1976. *A History of Baton Rouge, 1699-1812*. Baton Rouge: Louisiana State University Press.

Moore, Michael and Lynda Moore, 1997. "Fall from Grace: Implications of the O.J. Simpson rial for Postmodern Criminal Justice," *Sociological Spectrum* 17: 305- 322.

Multi-Agency Homicide Task Force. 2003a. Press Release of May 26.

———. 2003b. Agency web page available online at: http://brgov.com/TaskForce

Mustafa, Susan, Tony Clayton and Sue Israel. 2006. *I've Been Watching You: The South Louisiana Serial Killer*. Bloomington, IN: Author House.

Noel, Josh. 2003. "Police Statement on Lee Contradicts Early Reports," *Baton Rouge Advocate*, November 13.

Noel, Josh and Emily Kern. 2003a. "Professor Says Family 'Very Certain' It's Yoder." *Baton Rouge Advocate*, March 14.

———. 2003b. "Carrie Yoder's Body Found in Whiskey Bay," *WBRZ*, March 14.

Pitchford, Roy. 2005. "Gillis Pleads Not Guilty." *Baton Rouge Advocate*. July 10.

Rosenau, Pauline. 1992. *Postmodernism and the Social Sciences*. Princeton: Princeton University Press.

Rosenblatt, Susannah and James Rainey, 2005. "Katrina Rumors," *Los Angeles Times*, September 27.

Schneckloth v. Bustamonte. 1973. 418 U.S. 218.

Second Annual Louisiana Sexual Assault Conference. 2004. "Where is the Outrage? Spon sored by the Louisiana Foundation Against Sexual Assault, Baton Rouge, December 8- 10.

Shnayerson, Michael. 2006. "The Net's Mater Data-Miner." Vanity Fair.com, available online at http://www.vanityfair.com, accessed September 5.

Smelser, Neil. 1963. *Theory of Collective Behavior*, New York: Free Press of Glencoe.

Stanley, Stephanie. 2006. An Invisible Man. New York: Berkley Books.

———. 2003. "BR Women Convert Anger to Action." *New Orleans Times Picayune*, March 18.

Strinati, Dominic. 2000. *An Introduction to the Study of Popular Culture*. London: Routledge.

Tucci, Ken and Jan Worthington. 1990. *The Mad Housers: Shelters for the Homeless.* Princeton: Films for the Humanities and Science.

Turner, James. 2005. "Shooting Prompts Additional Safety," *The Southern Digest,* October 18.,

WDSU. 2003a. "Englade's Book Idea Not Sitting Well With Families," November 13.

———. 2003b. "Baton Rouge Billboards Urge Vigilance," March 26.

Wecht, Cyril and Mark Curriden. 2005. *Tales from the Morgue.* Amherst, NY: Prometheus Books.

Weeber, Stan. Forthcoming. *Targeted Violence in Academe: A Critical Approach.* Transaction Publishers.

———. 2005. "Targeted Violence, Collective Behavior and Criminology: The D.C. Sniper Case," *Virginia Social Science Journal,* 40, Winter: 1-17.

Wiltz, Sue and Maurice Godwin. 2004. *Slave Master.* New York: Pinnacle.

Zugibe, Frederick. 2005. *Dissecting Death.* New York: Broadway Books.

Index

A

Adams, Detra 73
Adams, Jacqueline 26,111
Adams, Ricky 38,54
Alexander, Diane 84-86,106

B

Baden, Michael 27,111
Baton Rouge Advocate 13,76,111
Baton Rouge Recreation and Park
  Commission (BREC) 32,42,111
Benge, Rob 83
Blouin, Christina 92
Boisfontaine, Eugenie 37,73
Bowers, Tammy 73
Bowie, Letha 74
Bradley, Keisha 74
Breaux Bridge, Louisiana 84
Breeland, Ingrid 74
Brinkley, Douglas 26,111

Bryan, Ann 73
Bundy, Ted 9
Burns, Kari 13,111
Burt, Mona 75

C

Capers, Tina 73
Caraway, Steve 23
Carl's Jr. Hamburgers 95,101
Carter, Patricia 73
Carver, Alicia 74
Cataldie, Louis 6-7,12-13,18-19,46-
  47,54,61,90,95,97-98,108,111
Causey, Lora 74
CBS Evening News 27-28,111
CBS News 28,112
Church of Christ 38
Citizens Against Senseless Killings 92

Citizens Against the Serial Killer
  (CASK) 53,56-57,60-61,63-64,68,92
City Confidential 12,112
City Social (Baton Rouge, LA) 2
Clayton, Tony 3,114
CNN 28,112
Cobb, Sylvia 74
Colomb, Dene 7,11,25,36-
  37,41,46,51-53,57,60,72,74,86
Connie Chung 16
Courtney, Veronica 74
Court TV 41,48,53
Cox Cable 33
Crime Library 13,87-88,112
Curriden, Mark 27,115

D

Daigle, Christina 73
Daigre, April 73
Darensbourg, Elizabeth 73
Davis, Leslie 94-95
Davis, Lisa 92-94
Dee, Lisa 93
Deville, Elizabeth 73
D'Iberville, Sieur 5
DeSoto, Geralyn 11-12,37,65,74,84,86
Dobie, Ann 12,112
Duke, David 98
Dunn, Antoinette 75
Durden, Priscilla 74

E

East Carolina University 16
EBay 31
Edwards, Florida 73
Edwards, Monique 74
Emmert, Mark 60
Englade, Pat 16,34,52,67-68,89-
  90,95,103-106

F

Fayetteville, North Carolina 16,47
Federer, Kassie 37,73
Finch, Susan 43,112
Flarity, Rachel 14,112
FOX News 9
FOX News Live 16
Fowler, Mary Ann 74
Fund, John 112

G

Gaudet, Marcia 112
George, John 112
Geraldo Rivera 16
Gerbner, George 113
Gilcrease, Teresa 74
Gillis, Sean Vincent 84,90,103
Godawa, Mary Ann 62,64-65
Godwin, Maurice 2-3,14,16-19,24-
  25,30,32,39,41,45,47-49,52-56,62-
  63,68,71,75-76,82-83,87,89-91,94-
  97,99-105,107,113
Godwin Trial and Forensic
  Consultancy 16
Goffman, Erving 113
Greater Baton Rouge Business Report
  113
Green, Consandra 96
Green, Cynthia 73
Green, Gina Wilson 7,9,16-17,19,24-
  25,32,34-36,46,59,65,72,74,82-
  83,86
Green River Killer 9
Gremillion, Robin 74
Guidry, Cennea 74
Gunn, Robert 113
Gyan, Joe 113

H

Hallcox, Jarrett 113
Harbor, Riley 53

Hardball 16
Haselden, Debra Ann 73
Hawkins, Patricia 74
Hayes, Tawanda Renee 74
Haygood, Wil 113
Henslin, James 113
Highway 90 107
Hollingsworth, Nelvil 85
Houma (Indians) 5
Hunt, Deborah 73

I

Indiana State University 16
Israel, Sue 3

J

Jackson Patricia Ann 73
Jackson, Paul 113
Jackson, Terry 73
Jehovah's Witnesses 38-40
Johnson, Allen 113
Jones, Griezelda 73

K

KATC 113
Kenner, Louisiana 23
Kern, Emily 13
Kinamore, Pam 7,18-19,24-26,30,35-
    37,46,52,59-60,63,65,72,74,82,85-
    86
Klandermans, Bert 113
Kretzer, Karl 113
Krummel, Linda 75
Kuntz, Mary 30,41

L

Lacour, Barbara Ann 74
Lafayette Utilities System 33
Lake Charles, Louisiana 83
LaVigne, Jeannie 72

Lee, Derrick Todd 1-3,5-7,9-
    12,37,40,67,71-72,75-76,81-86,89-
    90,92,94-96,97,99,101,103-107
Lee, Jacqueline 81-82
Lee High School (Baton Rouge,
    Louisiana) 41
Lirette, Leon 107
Louisiana Secretary of State's Office
    106
Louisiana State University 35-38,49-
    50,53-54,60-62,68,77-78
Louisiana Superdome 98
Louisiana Supreme Court 11,106

M

Malvo, Lee Boyd 5
Mandeville, Louisiana 22
Marino, Lynne 18,20,24
Masamichi, Inoue 113
McCutcheon, Leroy 32
McDonald, James 112
McGhee, Melinda 7
Mebruer, Michael 96
Mebruer, Randi 95-97
Methodist College (North Carolina) 16
Meyers, Rose 114
Mikell, Shirley 73
Miller, Rebecca 74
Mixon, Danny 96-97,99,104,106
Montz, Melissa 72
Moore, Lynda 114
Moore, Michael 114
Morgan, Monica 74
MSNBC 16
Muhammad, John 5
Mustafa, Susan 114

N

Natchez, Mississippi 7
Neustrom, Mike 25
Nevils, Marilyn 74
Newman, Rene 75

Noel, Josh 114

O

Odom, James 96,98,106
Odom, Joel 97
O'Neal, Sheila 94

P

Pace, Charlotte Murray 7,11-12,17-
    19,24-25,32,35,37,46,52,59-
    61,65,72,75
Parker, Eleanor 72
Parks, Rosa 15
Pate, Lisa 74
Patin, Pamela 74
Piglia, Ed 104
Pitchford, Roy 114
Platt, Bill 7
Psycho-Geographic Profiling 17-18

Q

R

Rainey, James 114
Rankins, Rosalyn 73
Ready Portions Meat (Baton Rouge,
Louisiana) 65
Reigal, Louis 60
Richardson, Lakisha 73
Robinson, Chad 91
Robinson, Lillian 74
Roman Catholic Church 37
Rosenau, Pauline 101,114
Rosenblatt, Susannah 114

S

Salters, Jippari 73
Sauerwin, Charlotte 72
Schmidt, Hardee 74
Shelvin, Shannon 73

Shnayerson, Michael 114
Shorts, Leroy 96-97
Sinquefield, John 85
Slovak, Mark 39
Smelser, Neil 114
Smith, Jackie Lynn 73
South Louisiana Highway Killer 107
Stanford, Gloria 73
Stanley, Stephanie 114
Stanton, Lee 6
Strinati, Dominic 114
St. Martin's Parish, Louisiana 69-71
Stokes, Janice 73

T

Tanner, Gloria 74
Taylor, Joyce 73
Teasley, Geri 68
Thibodeaux, Danielle 74
Thomas, Claretha 73
Trevecca Nazarene University
    (Tennessee) 16
Tucci, Ken 115
Turner, James 115

U

United Parcel Service 31-33
University of Liverpool 16
USENET 102

V

Vance-Granville Community College
    (North Carolina) 16
Van Der Wielen, Jos 26
Voung, Muoi 74

W

Walker, Jessica 74
Walker, Sondra Kathy 74
Walker, Tannis 74

Wall Street Journal 68
Warner, Connie 95-96
WDSU 115
Wecht, Cyril 115
Weeber, Stan 115
White, Ed 52
Wilcox, Laird 112
Williams, Diana 73
Williams, Diana Marie 74
Williams, Joyce 74
Wiltz, Sue 115
Woods, Datrell 107
Worthington, Jan 115

X

Y

Yoder, Carrie Lynn 3,7-8,12,36,42,45-79
Yoder, Dave 61
Yoder, Steve 71-72

Z

Zugibe, Frederick 115

www.ingramcontent.com/pod-product-compliance
Lightning Source LLC
Chambersburg PA
CBHW021145070326
40689CB00044B/1133